INSTRUCTOR'S MANUAL

ACCENT

Conversational French One   Fourth Edition

ROBERT M. TERRY
University of Richmond

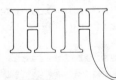

Heinle & Heinle Publishers, Inc.
Boston, Massachusetts 02210

TABLE DES MATIERES

ANSWERS TO WRITTEN EXERCISES

SAMPLE TESTS 141

INTRODUCTION

The fourth edition of **Accent**: Conversational French One is a new book; the grammar discussions found in the earlier edition remain, forming the core of a totally restructured and refurbished text. **Accent** presents a complete four-skills approach to learning French plus an innovative look at culture.

There are two major focuses of **Accent**:

1. The mastery-based study of a manageable corpus of linguistic features of French.
2. The functionally based use of the language, which allows learners to use the linguistic features for active, spontaneous self-expression.

To this end, the scope of grammatical features has been limited to those features that are fundamental to effective communication at the beginning language level. Numerous exceptions to rules of use have been removed and the order of presentation of the grammar corpus has been rearranged to approximate a logical sequence of introduction based on frequency of use and the development of thought.

Similarly, all model sentences and exercises have been changed to reflect this new structure. Most exercises are based on realistic situations that call for active student participation and personalized, natural language use. Exercises are long enough to allow for sufficient practice on the structure being studied but brief enough not to be boring.

All **Situations** have been rewritten and for the most part are based on situations in which a language learner might find him or herself, and which illustrate certain cultural features that are sources of inter-cultural differences and cross-cultural misunderstandings. Further study of the cultural feature in question is advanced through a series of questions in English (**Qu'en savez-vous?**), which prompt a deeper examination of that feature, calling on logical deduction and general knowledge. The following books might prove helpful as source books for cultural information:

Hilton, Lynn M., ed. France: Its People and Culture. Lincolnwood, IL: National Textbook Company, 1978 (No. 9525-6).

Levno, Arley W. Rencontres culturelles: Cross-cultural mini-dramas. Lincolnwood, IL: National Textbook Company, 1977 (No. 1247-4).

Michaud, G. and G. Torrès. Nouveau guide France. Paris: Hachette (National Textbook Company, No. 1928-2).

Miller, J. Dale and Maurice Loiseau. USA-France Culture Capsules. Salt Lake City: Culture Contrasts Co.

Quénelle, G. and J. Tournaire. La France dans votre poche. Paris: Hatier, 3rd edition.

Visages du Québec. Lincolnwood, IL: National Textbook Company (No. 1118-4).

Pronunciation features necessary for accurate oral production and for listening discrimination are included in the text and in the **Partie orale** of the **Cahier d'exercices.**

The corpus of vocabulary presented in this fourth edition is practical and useful. Glossing of words is innovative; new active and passive vocabulary items in the **Situations** are distinguished and glossed with the text. Active vocabulary is printed in boldface in the **Situations**, in the **Mots clefs,** in the grammar presentations, and in the French/ English glossary at the end of the book. Passive vocabulary items, on the other hand, are indicated with a degree mark in the **Situations** and glossed in the margins. Those vocabulary items not printed in boldface in the text are considered passive vocabulary, which may be made active at the instructor's discretion. Only the active vocabulary as indicated in the textbook is used in the exercises forming the corpus of the **Cahier d'exercices.** Lists of all active vocabulary items in each chapter are included in the Instructor's Manual **(Mots en action)** and may be reproduced and distributed to students. The end-of-book glossary contains all words used in the text except true cognates, and all active vocabulary items are indicated in boldface. In each of the chapter discussions in this instructor's manual additional vocabulary is suggested--vocabulary relating to the theme of the **Situation** or to topical vocabulary introduced in the lesson. This supplementary vocabulary is not included in the textbook glossaries.

Many chapters contain short vocabulary lists **(Les Mots clefs)** comprised of topical terms or representative groups of grammar words (verbs, adjectives, adverbs, etc.). These lists are not exhaustive but represent high-frequency vocabulary items relative to the point under discussion. Most vocabulary lists are followed by an exercise **(Autrement dit),** which is lexical in nature and not grammar-based. Many words in these lists are not included in the active vocabulary and are considered passive items. At the instructor's discretion certain items may be included in the students' active vocabulary.

A **Lecture** follows every three lessons. The content of the **Lectures** is new and novel. Selections are presented that highlight certain aspects of **le monde francophone.** The exercises accompanying each **Lecture** bring into focus the cultural content of the passage and also train students in the development of reading skills--contextual guessing, word families, and reading for comprehension and not for memorization of factual data. Activities are suggested for further investigation of the topic of the **Lecture.**

A **Révision** follows each **Lecture.** The **Révision** exercises and activities focus on fundamental structures studied in the preceding lessons--on those structures vital to the communicative effort. In the **Révisions,** as in many other exercises, previously learned grammar points are reintegrated for review and practice. Each **Révision** includes ten sentences for translation into French.

The **Cahier d'exercices** is an integral component of this project, since it includes practice in the development of writing and listening comprehension skills, while the textbook is basically directed toward grammar presentations and the development of speaking and reading skills. Cultural information pervades both books. Exercises in the **Cahier d'exercices** may be used effectively for homework, for reinforcing material studied in class, and for providing additional practice at each stage of learning. Each written exercise is keyed to the appropriate section in each chapter where the point being drilled is discussed.

Accent and its ancillary materials provide both instructors and students with a complete program of elementary-level language study, based on the development of all four skills and an exposure to francophone culture with equal emphasis on all five areas, allowing individual instructors the flexibility to stress any specific area(s) more than others. This new program involves the students actively in all aspects of language learning and urges free, spontaneous use of the language at every stage, for it is only through using the language that a facility and functional proficiency can be developed.

How to use this book effectively

Sequencing

For courses meeting three times per week:

It is suggested that the instructor concentrate on lessons I-XXI and the accompanying **Révisions** and **Lectures**. This will provide students with a manageable core of grammar for functional language use even if they do not continue beyond this level of language study. A strong basic knowledge of grammatical structures can be built upon and refined at subsequent levels of study.

If a larger grammatical corpus is desired in the first year (chapters 1-23), several activities in the text may be omitted:

Lectures

Certain chapter components
1. Exercises (at the instructor's discretion)
2. **Formation et expression** (selected exercises)
3. **De l'oral à l'écrit**

If chapters 1-23 will form the corpus of study, it is suggested that nine chapters be studied during the first half of the course (+ **Révisions** and **Lectures**), affording time for a slower, more leisurely pace for extended work during the introductory chapters, thus assuring mastery and the development of a minimal proficiency during the first semester. In the second semester the remaining twelve lessons (+ **Révisions** and **Lectures**) can be more realistically assimilated once a technique for learning a second language is developed and the essentials of grammar have been learned (verb person, number, and tense meanings; adjective agreement and position; basic negation and interrogation; the function of determiners). Later material is based on that material found in the first few chapters.

For courses meeting four or five times per week:

Obviously, with more class meetings per week, the instructor has at his or her disposal more time for directing class activities to provide students with additional practice using the material taught and the possible inclusion of chapters 22 and 23 (+ **Révision** and **Lecture**). Most, if not all, material provided in the textbook and accompanying **Cahier d'exercices** can be used to its full advantage without overburdening the student with too much material to be learned, assimilated, mastered, and put to functional use in too short a time.

Certain material may still be optional, at the instructor's discretion. Quality instruction of a manageable portion of material is much more important than overburdening students with a large quantity of material that cannot be put to use in the relatively short period of time available. Students should be provided with ample time for practice in developing both productive (speaking and writing) skills in loosely teacher-controlled situations and in the production of spontaneous second-language use.

General strategies

Instructors should avoid introducing too much material (including exceptions to grammar rules) that falls outside of the scope of material presented in the text. It must be kept in mind that elementary-level language study is primarily a skill-building stage in which the use of those skills is limited only by the corpus of grammar and vocabulary. Nonetheless, adequate practice in the active use of the skills being developed is crucial. Students should develop a facility in the manipulation of grammatical forms and ready recall and appropriate use of active vocabulary.

When drilling vocabulary and acquisition of new structures, correctness is extremely important. When the language is being used by students for communication, the appropriateness and degree of communication (passive through listening, active through production) are significantly more important. Error correction should be minimal during communicative activities. The instructor should assume the role of a passive listener and moderator during such periods of work. It is only through continuous, loosely monitored practice that a student can develop a comfortable facility in self-expression.

Requisite knowledge of materials previously learned should be reinforced before the introduction of new grammar points. For example, before introducing the position of adjectives in French, the gender and number of nouns and adjective agreement must be reviewed. Time spent reviewing previously taught material is never wasted time, since students will begin to see the cumulative nature of language learning and the necessity for the cyclical reintegration of content matter.

Instructors should make all efforts, in the course of the introduction of new materials, to express the grammatical concept in his or her own words, using the explanantion in the textbook as a guide and the model sentences as the basis for the explanation. The "rule" is based on usage; the model sentences illustrate the grammar concept in actual use.

Exercises can frequently be used as **points de départ** for short exchanges between the instructor and student. For instance, in an item such as **Aimez-vous la musique?** (in which the use of the definite article in making generalized statements is being drilled), the instructor might ask:

a. Quelle musique aimez-vous? La musique classique? pop?
b. Avez-vous une collection de disques?
c. Préférez-vous les disques ou les cassettes?
d. Avez-vous une chaîne-stéréo?
e. Préférez-vous écouter la radio ou votre chaîne-stéréo? Pourquoi?

In such a conversation, fragment sentences or simple **oui** or **non** answers are quite acceptable since such features comprise the bulk of everyday oral communication. It is natural, realistic, and an opportunity for the student to talk about him or herself and no longer a formal, structural grammar exercise. Personalization of all activities, where possible, is one of the most effective teaching and testing strategies. The student is no longer a passive listener and an infrequent participant in relatively unexciting (but vital) exercises, but becomes actively involved, while often unaware of being so, in meaningful grammar-based activities that include the needed practice in using what has been learned.

Any use of authentic realia enhances the learning process, providing a concrete link between the vocabulary item being learned and its true "cultural" form, and most often removes the artificial native-language translation equivalent. The importance of the use of real materials lies primarily in affording the students the opportunity to see and handle bits of French culture, as sometimes insignificant as they might appear, shifting the focus of learning from the artificiality of the classroom situation to the reality and vitality of what they are studying.

A relaxed, nonthreatening classroom atmosphere is most conducive to effective foreign-language instruction and learning. Many elements that inhibit willing active participation are removed. Language learning can and should be enjoyable--and will be--if students are at ease in their efforts to learn, to assimilate, to practice, and to demonstrate their developing skills and abilities.

Communication is a cooperative venture. When possible, the seating arrangement of the classroom should not be in the traditional row and line, but in a semicircle in which students can actually see the speaker and can respond directly to the partner in communication and not to the back of his or her head or to the instructor alone.

Small-group work has proved to be very effective in fostering a free exchange between students without fear of committing errors and being corrected in front of peers. The instructor may circulate among the groups, monitoring their work and providing reinforcement or help when needed.

Lectures should not be used solely for the repetition of factual data found in the text, but as springboards for further activities, limited only by the instructor's imagination. The cultural information found in the **Lectures** can lead to exciting activities based on the theme of the lesson. The **Lectures** should not be studied as vehicles for grammar but as (1) devices for the development of the reading skill using contextual clues and guessing in a continuous passage, recognition of word families, and implications of meaning and (2) sources for cultural information (both francophone and cross-cultural) for study and discussion.

Révisions have been placed after every three lessons. For formal testing and evaluation, the amount of material is of manageable proportions, yet diverse enough to provide variety in the composition of test items and student responses. Exercises in the **Révisions** are built around the major aspects of grammar introduced in the three preceding chapters. Use of the **Révisions** is crucial to the learning and reinforcement of the grammar studied.

The written drills in the **Cahier d'exercices** provide ample practice in exercises ranging from mechanical drill to translation and free composition. These exercises may be used as daily homework for evaluation or for in-class work.

The **Partie orale** in the **Cahier d'exercices** is an evaluative or practice component based on the development of the listening skill. Much listening comprehension practice is carried out in class through routine conversation and drill. Verification of accuracy in listening is carried out through language laboratory work in which the subtleties of the language must be discerned without seeing the speaker.

A typical chapter: rationale and strategies

Situation. The **Situation** serves as an introduction to specific facets of French culture whose theme is used in many exercises in the chapter and as an inductive introduction to the grammar points of the chapter. Both active vocabulary items used throughout the chapter and passive vocabulary items are glossed, thus allowing the use of the **Situation** as an overture to the lesson.

The **Situations** are not written as dialogues to be memorized, but they may be used for practice in reading aloud or for role playing.

Instructors should take full advantage of all opportunities presented in the **Situation** to bring in additional materials--realia, relevant minidramas, and culture capsules, among other items--to present a well-rounded, complete view of the point of culture under discussion and not a distorted, stereotypical picture based on generalizations. Sources of cross-cultural conflict or variation must be pointed out, since most American students have a very stilted, prejudiced view of their own culture, and an overly generalized view of foreign cultures.

Some instructors may prefer to use the **Situation** at the conclusion of a unit of study rather than at the beginning. The flexibility of **Accent** allows either sequence, although the glossing assumes that the **Situation** opens the lesson.

A ce propos. This section singles out certain structures or vocabulary items that cause problems for language learners - prepositions and verbs in particular. Most of these items appear in the **Situation** but may not appear in the discussions of grammar or in the exercises. The instructor should decide if the information in this section should be active or passive.

Qu'en savez-vous? This section begins with a brief discussion of the point of culture, which is followed by approximately ten questions based on this point. **Qu'en savez-vous?** is written in English, since students at this level have an extremely restricted active corpus of grammar and vocabulary and would find attempts at discussion in French very frustrating (as would the instructor). To provide opportunities for unhampered discussion of culture--both French and American--all obstacles that would thwart students have been removed. Questions are thought-provoking and call on the students' store of general knowledge and acquired attitudes rather than on the parroting back of memorized factual data. Logical deduction is also called upon in answering many of these questions. Discussion need not end with the questions provided, but will be limited only by the creativity of the instructor.

Prononciation. This chapter component is based on selected phonetic phenomena of French, and in no way pretends to be a complete picture of the sounds of French. Those features that can lead to misunderstandings due to mispronunciation are studied and examined. Included are features such as liaison, the mute **e**, and practice in spelling. Keep in mind that beginning-level students rarely approach "near native"--not in pronunciation, not in fluency. Correction in pronunciation should never supersede efficacy in communication, unless pronunciation errors hinder comprehension or unless the focus of a particular activity is pronunciation per se. This section is duplicated in the **Cahier d'exercices** and on the language laboratory tapes for additional practice.

Grammaire et exercices. This is the core of each lesson. Grammar points are discussed in manageable portions and illustrated with several model sentences. Where feasible, students should be encouraged to deduce the grammar principle from the model sentences and state the principle in their own words. Verification is carried out by comparing the two principles: the students' and that in the text.

Instructors should feel no compulsion to finish the **Grammaire et exercices** in one class meeting. A measured pace with significant practice should be central. Too much material presented too fast with too little time for assimilation is totally ineffective.

The exercises are presented in a developmental sequence--from mechanical manipulative drills to less controlled, more spontaneous and creative exercises calling for active application of the grammatical principle. Certain exercises are culturally seeded, i.e., they offer further glimpses of culture, which should be used to their fullest advantage. Students should participate in all exercises according to the model, since each exercise is designed to elicit use of certain grammatical structures.

Schematics provided in the text (time lines, charts, etc.) should be drawn on the blackboard or on an overhead projector to aid students in interpreting text illustrations during periods of preparation, individual study, and review. Additional model sentences are helpful but should be planned before presentation to the class.

Some exercises may be used for written practice rather than for oral drilling in class, although exercises specifically designed to be written are found in the **Cahier d'exercices.**

Students should be encouraged to speak up during oral practice, and to look at the other participant(s) in the exercise. The situational frame for each exercise should be kept in mind, since the items are most meaningful when kept in the proper context. The language in the exercises is real authentic language in a logical framework, and participation in the activity should be treated as such.

Formation et expression. This portion of each chapter serves as an end-of-chapter review and provides new exercises to be used as in-class evaluative devices. It would be appropriate for this review session to occur on the day following completion of study of the grammar core of the chapter.

Exercices de contrôle. These exercises concentrate on the major aspects of those grammar principles studied in the lesson.

Causons un peu. This section includes personalized questions based on active language use of the grammar studied plus the theme of the **Situation.** As in the effective use of all exercises, do not let any opportunity pass for a follow-up conversation with the student(s) involved using the original question as a point of departure. Students should be encouraged but not forced to answer in complete sentences, since this exercise is based on the demonstration of mastery for the purpose of communication, and real-language use should be emphasized.

De l'oral à l'écrit. The concluding activties in each chapter free the students from strong teacher-controlled activities and offer the opportunity to use newly learned structures and vocabulary in realistic student-centered and student-generated situations.

Pour parler. This section offers a chance for free use of spoken language calling for inclusion of the grammar principles of the chapter. Most of the activities in this section involve role-playing. Students should be urged to be creative in assuming their roles and should not be allowed to use notes or to memorize their roles. According to the situation, students should act out the scene before the class and not from their seats. Naturalness and spontaneity are the key to the effective use of **Pour parler,** for it is the obvious goal of language study: the use of language (including sounds and gestures) in unexpected situations for the purpose of communicating effectively with others.

Pour écrire. This is an activity specifically designed for relatively uncontrolled student composition based on a given topic. It is obvious that the students should attempt to incorporate as many of the structures studied as is feasible.

Evaluating student performance

Test what you teach. Evaluation of student performance should follow and be based on the techniques used in teaching the material. Furthermore, evaluative components should be weighted according to the amount of emphasis placed on the development of each of the skill areas. For example, if the speaking skill receives one quarter of the emphasis in class instruction and practice, it should similarly comprise one quarter of the evaluation. Speaking should be tested by having students evaluated through oral performance and not in writing.

If indeed the ultimate goal of foreign language study is to provide the student with the ability to use the language, he or she must be given the opportunity to produce what has been learned in relatively unstructured situations calling for creative language use. To lead to such free language use, mastery must first be determined through demonstration of the knowledge of the mechanics of the language. Such mastery can be evaluated through the use of mechanical exercises, such as the following:

a. Basic sentence transformations
   1. Rewrite the following sentences in the negative (interrogative, etc.).
   2. Rewrite the following sentences inserting the adjectives given in the correct form and position.
b. Fill-in-the-blank
   1. Fill in the blank with the appropriate form of the present indicative of the infinitive given.
   2. Fill in the blank with the appropriate form of the demonstrative adjective.
c. Substitution
   1. Rewrite the following sentences substituting direct object pronouns for the object nouns.
   2. Combine the following pairs of sentences using the appropriate relative pronoun. Make all necessary changes.

Evaluation of creative, functional language use is best carried out through personalized or open-ended activities in which students react or answer appropriately to items which, although seeded for specific grammatical forms, allow self-expression. Structures and vocabulary items that have been mastered and that students can use effectively should be included. Such items might include the following:

a. Determiners. Complete each of the following sentences with the appropriate definite, indefinite, or partitive article + noun.
   1. Voici trois choses que j'aime: ___, ___ et ___.
   2. Dans ma chambre, il y a ___, ___ et ___.
   3. Pour Noël, j'ai reçu ___, ___ et ___.

b. Interrogatives. Following is an interview in which all the questions are missing. Create an appropriate question that would elicit the answer given.

   Paul: Bonjour, David. _____?
   David: Oui, ça va bien, merci. _____?
   Paul: Pas mal. _____?
   David: Oui, je voudrais bien t'accompagner au concert. _____?
   Paul: Il commence à 20h30.

c. Complete the following sentences.
   1. Si clauses.
      (a) Si j'avais $1 000, _____.
      (b) J'irai en France cet été si _____.
      (c) J'aurais reçu une bonne note si _____.
   2. Subjunctive.
      (a) Mes parents ont peur que je _____.
      (b) Mon (ma) camarade de chambre veut que je _____.
      (c) Après la classe, il faut que je _____.

d. Answer the following personal questions.
   1. Negatives.
      (a) Etes-vous jamais allé(e) en Chine?
      (b) Qui vous a aidé avec vos devoirs?

2. Object pronouns.
   (a) Avez-vous vu le film "E.T."? Comment avez-vous trouvé ce film?
   (b) Quand écrivez-vous à vos parents?

e. Compositions.
   1. Imperatives. Give me clear instructions on how to make a sandwich.
   2. Imperfect tense. What did you use to do every day before leaving for school?

Such activities should be evaluated based on (1) grammaticality, (2) appropriateness, and (3) communicability, with emphasis on the latter two aspects since such items call for the use of language as a true communicative instrument and not solely as a mechanical exercise.

Students must practice such activities throughout the course of study and not be exposed to them for the first time on formal tests and examinations.

In the following pages you will find teaching and testing suggestions and strategies for each grammar chapter in the book, including

a. The structures covered in the chapter
b. Objectives for the chapter
c. Rationale for both the **Situation** and the **Grammaire**
d. Strategies for both the **Situation** and the **Grammaire**
e. Testing suggestions
f. Additional Materials

Also included are

a. Sample tests for each group of three chapters + the **Révision**.
b. Answers to written exercises in the **Cahier d'exercices** excluding those exercises calling for personal answers. (These exercises are indicated in the **Cahier** with an asterisk.) In the sentence translations, not all possibilities are indicated, but the translations given provide the basic structures called for in the English sentence.
c. Suggested translations for those exercises in each **Révision**.

A tapescript for all oral exercises in the **Cahier d'exercices** is available upon request from the publisher.

Chapitre Préliminaire

Objectives

To introduce students to French through the recognition of cognates

To illustrate the discrepancies between spoken and written French through the repetition and reading of cognates

To use contextual clues and intelligent guessing to discern the meanings of unknown words

To provide students with lists of expressions that are commonly used in class by both the teacher and students

Rationale

The **Chapitre Préliminaire** is an introduction to French. Most students are aware that English has a strong French influence in its vocabulary. English and French are not phonetic languages—what is perceived through reading rarely resembles what is heard. Therefore the **Chapitre préliminaire** begins with a dehydrated story composed mainly of cognates that students are to read...more than likely with a high degree of understanding.

Next appears a list of cognates which, if read, are quite recognizable. Students are asked to repeat the words as modeled on the tape program or by the instructor. If students are allowed to look at the words as they repeat them, chances are much greater for error, i.e., they will most likely pronounce the words as if they were the English "look-alikes," ignoring the true French pronunciation. Here, as throughout the book, it is advisable not to let students perform oral exercises and activities with their books open, but to react to the situation given without the often misleading sight/sound correlation.

When the opening dehydrated story is "fleshed out" into a complete dialogue, students can still derive the gist of the reading through the use of cognates, contextual clues, and intelligent guessing. The exercise following the dialogue leads students to use textual and contextual clues in completing the meaning of the material. This technique of reading or understanding materials using clues can be used with the **Situations** and **Lectures** throughout __Accent__, and proves more effective than having the instructor tell students word meanings. Such learning strategies can be elicited from the students in the course of class work and discussion and might help other students in developing second language learning skills.

Students should be told from the outset that they are not expected to sound French, but that through training and consistent practice they will gradually acquire an acceptable (albeit not perfect) pronunciation and a certain facility in recognizing and using forms, structures, and vocabulary necessary for oral and written communication.

As students acquire a larger working knowledge of French, including sufficient grammar structures and vocabulary, most classroom interchange can be in French except for the formal presentation and discussion of grammar. To this end there is included in the **Chapitre préliminaire** a list of expressions of (1) what the instructor might say and (2) what the student might say. While not exhaustive lists, the most commonly used and needed expressions are included. As the need progresses, more expressions can be added.

Strategies

Have students mention French words in common use in English. Make a list of the words on the board or on an overhead projector. Give the true French pronunciation of words and have students repeat them.

Have students bring in advertising or articles containing French words.

To test general knowledge of France and the French language, ask
  where France is located
  how big France is
  what countries France borders on
  where French is spoken
  where the francophone countries named are located
  what products we get from France.

To discuss and break down stereotypes, have students describe their personal views of France and the French. Ask why they hold such views. Now, ask them to describe the stereotypical American. Are such stereotypes and generalizations valid? Why (not)?

Have each student mention something French: a person, a place, a thing, an idea, an historical event, etc.

Chapitre Un

Structures

Gender of nouns

Plural of nouns

Indefinite article

Definite article

Voici, voilà, il y a

Avoir (to have): Present indicative

Subject pronouns

Contractions

Objectives

To understand that French nouns are masculine or feminine

To form regular plurals of nouns

To use forms of the indefinite article correctly

To use forms of the definite article correctly

To distinguish among the meanings of **voici, voilà,** and **il y a** and to use
them appropriately

To use the present indicative of **avoir** with correct correlation of
pronouns and verb forms

To make the correct contractions of **à** and **de** + definite articles

Rationale

Situation

Une ville française Demonstrating the ability to ask for, get, and
give directions is a very realistic, natural use of language. This
introduction to a French city not only approximates real language use
but introduces the student to the cultural differences between his or
her own and foreign cities.

Grammaire

An understanding of the essential features of French nouns--gender and the formation of regular plural forms--is basic to subsequent work and requisite for verb and adjective agreement. Definite and indefinite articles are common gender and number markers and must be used appropriately, as in English. Confusion can result from false parallels drawn between English (there is, there are) and the dual French counterparts (voilà, il y a). The French conjugation system exhibits various verb forms in the different persons. Similarly, subject pronoun usage, while closely parallel to that of English, varies markedly in the third persons singular and plural due to the lack of a neuter gender and the use of a pronoun as both personal and nonpersonal. Contraction in French occurs with prepositions and definite articles as opposed to contraction with the verb in English. It is not determined by style in French, but is a normal phenomenon in all styles and levels of language.

Strategies

Situation

Students may be asked to give directions on campus, in town, or in another city using available maps.

Cultural study of foreign cities and comparison with various American cities may be carried out.

Using photos or illustrations of streets in foreign cities, ask students how they know they are not American cities.

Grammaire

Using new vocabulary, students may be asked to indicate gender and/or number by recognizing oral clues of gender: **le, la, les; un, une, des.**

Make sure students understand that use of the appropriate definite or indefinite article is not indiscriminate but is based on usage parallel to English: the indefinite article introduces a new, not previously mentioned person or thing; the definite article, a specific person or thing that has already been mentioned.

Drill work is important at this stage on the distinction between **voici** and **voilà**, which point out, and **il y a**, which states the existence of something or someone, a distinction that does not exist in English.

It is important to practice subject pronoun substitution and obligatory verb agreement: J'ai une voiture. (il, nous, elles, tu, on, vous)

Include preliminary training on possession and contractions:

Voilà la voiture de la dame. (monsieur, voisin, aimi, garçon)
Paul va au théâtre. (musée, hôpital, café, églises)

Testing

Testing at this stage must be totally mechanical manipulation of grammatical features and recognition of vocabulary items due to the minimal amount of content matter.

Additional materials

Maps of French cities

Photos and illustrations of various buildings, streets, and locations in French cities

Vocabulary

il/elle va	he/she is going
il/elle est	he/she/it is

Mots en action

à côté de beside
l'agent (m) de police police officer
allez go
l'ami (m), l'amie (f) friend
l'avenue (f) avenue
avoir to have
la banque bank
bon, bonne good
le, la camarade de chambre roommate
le café café
le centre middle; downtown
le cinéma movies
continuez keep on, continue
le copain, la copine friend, pal
d'accord okay
la dame woman, lady
dans in (inside of)
derrière behind
deux two
devant in front of
à droite to the right, on the right
tout droit straight ahead
l'école (f) school
l'église (f) church
et and
la femme woman, wife
le garçon boy
gauche left
à gauche to the left, on the left
l'homme (m) man
l'hôpital (m) hospital
l'hôtel (m) hotel
le jardin garden
la jeune fille girl

jusqu'à up to, as far as
loin de far from
le lycée high school
Madame Ma'am
Mademoiselle Miss
le magasin store
la maison house
le marché market
Monsieur Sir
le monsieur man, gentleman
le musée museum
le parc park
la piscine swimming pool
la place (public) square
la plage beach
le plan map
la poste post office
près de near
le professeur teacher, professor
puis then, next
la résidence dormitory
la rue street
s'il vous plaît please
suivez follow, take
ta your
le théâtre theater
toi you
tournez turn
tout le monde everyone, everybody
l'université (f) university, college
la ville city, town
le voisin, la voisine neighbor
la voiture car, automobile

-15-

Structures

Possession (noun + **de** + possessor; **être à**)

Être (to be): present indicative

Cardinal numbers 0 to 10

Negation **(ne...pas)**

Yes-no questions (intonation change; **est-ce que**)

Objectives

To indicate possession using noun + **de** and **être à**

To use the verb **être** correctly in the present indicative

To recognize and use the cardinal numbers 0 to 10

To form basic negation using **ne...pas**

To form, ask, and answer yes-no questions using intonation change and **est-ce que**

Rationale

Situation

Deux conversations introduces students to levels of language (register) and formulae for greeting and leave taking. A semantic distinction such as **tu/vous** and its ramifications are extremely important for students to realize from the outset of their language-learning experience, since English lacks this distinction.

Grammaire:

Possession in French varies greatly from the English construction ('s). **Etre,** a verb of extreme high frequency and irregularity, like **avoir,** must be mastered from the outset, since both verbs form the basis for other tenses. Individuals are constantly confronted with numbers—as written digits and as they are spoken. Recognition of variant written forms and accurate perception and production of oral forms are crucial to information-seeking and giving. Negation is a very common phenomenon which, because of its form in French, must be mastered early. Correct placement of the negative particles and concomitant structural changes must be understood and mastered. Interrogation plays a major role in communication—information is sought or given as a result of it and conversations are maintained.

Yes-no questions comprise the largest group of interrogative
structures in actual usage, and intonation change and the use of **est-
ce que** are the forms most frequently used.

Strategies

Situation

Devise many various situations in which students must greet and say
good-bye to individuals of various social levels and degrees of
acquaintance: friends, peers, superiors, etc. Draw parallels, where
possible, with English, in which styles of spoken language vary with
the individuals being addressed.

Point out the differences in using **comment allez-vous?** and **ça va?, au
revoir** and **adieu, bonjour** and **salut;** the use of generic names for
items: **stylo/bic, réfrigérateur/frigo; vous/tu (toi);** greeting in
English (title + name) and greeting in French **(monsieur/madame/
mademoiselle** + title).

Grammaire

Use copious drilling on expressing possession in French to avoid the
potential transfer of the English pattern ('s) to French.

Point out the synonymity of indicating possession using noun + **de** +
noun and **être à.** Distinguish between **de qui...** (relationship) and **à
qui...** (possession).

Point out that **ce sont** is used with a third person plural noun,
although in current French, **c'est** is used in all circumstances.

Drill the conjugation of **être** in the present indicative. Then distinguish between **être** and **avoir** through listening comprehension and
speaking, especially the distinction **ils ont/ils sont** (liaison).

Numbers should be drilled based on correct production and
comprehension and not stressed in the written form since such usage is
not common (except in writing checks, for instance). Students should
be able to recognize and produce numbers readily without hesitation.
(Point out gestures to indicate numbers and the differences in
English.) Do not work with numbers in sequence since they are readily
memorized and not learned for spontaneous production.

Stress the correct placement of **ne...pas.** Point out the dual nature
of English negation (He doesn't have a book/He has no book) as
equivalent to the single French negation **(Il n'a pas de livre)** to
avoid insertion of the particle <u>do/does</u> in French. Emphasize the
change of **un, une, des** to **de** after a negative, since it is easily
forgotten.

Students should be drilled consistently on asking questions. Most classwork has been based on responding to teacher questions and students have great difficulty in forming questions due to a lack of practice. Play a game such as "Twenty Questions" to elicit yes-no questions from the students. Point out the use of **si** (yes). At this stage, the form of the question is secondary in importance to the appropriateness and relevance of the question vis à vis the information sought.

Testing

Testing should include listening comprehension activities based on
recognition of numbers
affirmative/negative
declaration/interrogation
être/avoir
responding to oral questions

Personalized items in which structures are controlled but student responses may vary must be used to evaluate mastery and control over structures and vocabulary in relatively free language use, e.g., **Avez-vous une voiture?**

Use a minimum of mechanical items that test mastery--this can be most effectively evaluated through in-class work, homework, and **Cahier d'exercices** activities.

Additional materials

Visuals representing descriptive adjectives

Labels for parts of the classroom

Pictures of individuals in conversation for guessing styles of language being used

Vocabulary

le bureau	office
le cours	course, subject
l'électrophone (m)	record player
l'élève (m, f)	(elementary) student, pupil
la lumière	light
le magnétophone	tape recorder
la mini-cassette	cassette recorder
la moquette	wall-to-wall carpeting
le mur	wall
le plafond	ceiling
le plancher	floor
le pupitre	(student) desk
le stylo feutre	felt-tip pen
le tapis	rug, carpet

la télévision television
le tourne-disque record player

Mots en action

alors well, then
l'anglais (m) English (language)
aujourd'hui today
au revoir good-bye
avoir tort to be wrong
le bic pen
bien well
assez bien pretty good
Je vais bien. I'm okay. I feel good.
bonjour hello; good morning,
   good afternoon
le bureau (teacher's) desk
le cahier (spiral, large) notebook)
calme calm
le carnet (pocket) notebook
ça va? How are you? (How's it going?)
ça va Okay. All right. Good.
C'est dommage. That's a shame. That's
   too bad.
la chaise chair
la chance luck
bonne chance good luck
la classe class
le Coca Coca-Cola, Coke
combien how much, how many
Comment allez-vous? How are you?
le crayon pencil
le devoir homework
le doigt finger
en in
enthousiaste enthusiastic
être to be
l'étudiant (m), l'étudiante
   (f) student
l'examen (m) test, examination

faible weak
fait (from faire) to make
la fenêtre window
le français French (language)
habile clever
jeune young
Je vais mal. I feel bad.
   I don't feel good.
la leçon lesson
levez raise
le livre book
mais but
malade sick, ill
Messieurs Gentlemen, Sirs
moins less, minus
la note mark, grade; note
le papier paper
pas mal Not bad
pauvre poor
la porte door
qui who, whom
riche rich
la salle de classe classroom
Salut! Hi!
stupide stupid
le stylo
(à bille) (ballpoint) pen
sympathique kind, nice
le tableau (black)board
tard late
A plus tard. See you later.
le travail work
triste sad

Chapitre Trois

Structures

Agreement of adjectives

Position of adjectives (following and preceding nouns; reduction of **des**
to **de**)

Regular conjugations

Present indicative of **-er** verbs

Verbs like **ouvrir**

Inverted questions (simple and complex)

Objectives

To make adjectives agree in gender and number with the noun(s) modified

To position adjectives correctly

To form and use correctly the present indicative of **-er** verbs and certain irregular verbs in **-ir** that follow the same pattern

To form questions using simple and complex inversion

Rationale

Situation

Arrivée en France presents a student who is arriving in France for the first time and who does not speak French well. Yet he manages to find his way by asking questions and getting directions from a **hôtesse d'accueil** at the airport. Certain important formulaic expressions that are extremely important for "decoding" messages are included: **Comment dit-on...? Que veut dire...?**

Grammaire:

The phenomenon of adjective agreement and position is introduced. The French system differs markedly from English, which exhibits invariable adjective form and a fixed pre-noun position. Regular conjugations are presented, pointing out stems and "standardized" endings to indicate tense and person. First conjugation (**-er**) verbs comprise the largest group of verbs in French and are the most regular in form. Understanding the basic concept that one conjugated verb form in French is equivalent to the three of the present tense in English is essential to avoid invented forms in French. The third major and most complex interrogative structure (inversion) is introduced. While simple inversion is relatively common, complex inversion is essentially not a conversational form but is found most frequently in formal writing and speaking; therefore it should be considered a structure for recognition.

Strategies

Situation

Students should be able to use **Comment dit-on...?** and **Que veut dire...?** readily in order to follow a conversation in French.

Point out pause sounds in French, e.g., **euh..**

Point out **vous désirez?** and **à votre service.**

Point out the importance of a **bureau d'accueil** and the **hôtesses** for information and directions.

Discuss the airports of Orly and Charles de Gaulle and how to get into Paris.

Point out the difference between **autocar** and **autobus.**

Grammaire

Adjectives, through agreement, frequently indicate the gender of the noun modified while the noun itself does not: **des voitures américaines.** Agreement must be stressed since English has no such system.

Emphasize that nouns of nationality are capitalized while adjectives are not.

Adjective position, being different from that of English, should be stressed. General descriptive adjectives usually follow the noun. The mnemonic device BANGS might be used for learning those adjectives that precede:

Beauty	beau, joli
Age	jeune, nouveau, vieux
Number	autre, cardinal and ordinal numbers
Goodness	bon, gentil, mauvais
Size	grand, gros, long, petit

The second situation in which **des** becomes **de** occurs when plural adjectives precede a noun.

Confusion between English and French verb usage often occurs in the present progressive form: I am listening; Are you playing? This concept must be drilled consistently from the outset to avoid the transfer of English patterns to French. Similarly, the occurrence of do/does, basically in negatives and interrogatives in English, could cause similar problems.

Point out the omission of the definite article when the name of a language directly follows **parler** or the preposition **en.**

Point out that verbs such as **ouvrir** follow first conjugation patterns only in the present indicative and in other verb forms derived from this tense: the imperfect and the present subjunctive.

Simple inverted questions are very common except in the first person singular where the use of **est-ce que** is preferred. Point out the use of the euphonic **t** in third person singular inversions. Stress the position of negative elements in inversion.

Complex inversion should be introduced and drilled but not be expected in active language use.

Testing

Listening comprehension activities including
  gender and adjective agreement
  position of adjectives
  declaration/inverted questions
  person of -er verbs

Mechanical items on adjective agreement and position; conjugation of -er verbs; transformation of declarative statements to questions with inversion

Personalized items using adjectives and verb forms

Additional materials

Photos of Orly and Charles de Gaulle airports, **hôtesses d'accueil**, Air France **autocar**, and tickets

Map of Paris, including airports

Color chart for paints, spectrum, etc.

Flags of nationalities included in text

Pictures illustrating descriptive adjectives

Pictures or examples of personal articles mentioned

Pictures illustrating actions of many -er verbs

Class schedule of a French student or French catalogue of courses

Vocabulary

l'allemand (m)	German (language)
la brosse à dents	toothbrush
le calcul intégral/différentiel	calculus
clair(e)	light (colors)
l'éducation physique (f)	physical education
l'espagnol (m)	Spanish (language)
foncé(e)	dark (colors)
la grammaire	grammar
l'italien (m)	Italian (language)
laisser	to leave; to allow, to let
le latin	Latin (language)
marron (invariable)	brown
orange (invariable)	orange
le peigne	comb
le russe	Russian (language)
les sciences politiques (fpl)	political science
le transistor	transistor radio
vif (vive)	bright (colors)
violet(te)	purple

Mots en action

l'aéroport (m) airport
aimer to like, to love
allemand, allemande German
apporter to bring
l'argent (m) money
arriver to arrive, to happen
l'autobus (m) bus (urban)
l'autocar (m) bus (interurban)
autre other
beau, belle pretty, handsome
belge Belgian
blanc, blanche white
bleu, bleue blue
la brosse brush
brun, brune brown
la chaîne stéréo stereo, record player
le chauffeur driver
la chaussure shoe
chercher to look for
chinois, chinoise Chinese
commander to order
Comment dit-on-- How do you say--
la comptabilité accounting
coûter to cost
découvrir to discover
demander to ask (for)
dépenser to spend (money)
désirer to want, to desire
détester to hate
difficile difficult, hard
donner to give
écouter to listen (to)
emprunter to borrow
entrer (dans) to enter
espagnol, espagnole Spanish
étranger, étrangère foreign
facile easy
fermer to close
fort, forte strong
gagner to earn, to win
gentil, gentille kind, nice
grand, grande big, tall
gris, grise gray
gros, grosse big, fat
habiter to live at, in; to inhabit
historique historical
honnête honest
il faut (+ verb) it is necessary to
intéressant, intéressante interesting

japonais, japonaise Japanese
jaune yellow
le jean (a pair of) blue jeans
joli, jolie pretty, beautiful
jouer to play
laid, laide ugly
la langue language
long, longue long
maigre thin, skinny
maintenant now
manger to eat
manquer to miss
marcher to walk
la matière subject
mauvais, mauvaise bad
méchant, méchante bad, ill-behaved
montrer to show
la musique music
nager to swim
noir, noire black
nouveau, nouvelle new
offrir to offer
ou or
oublier to forget
ouvrir to open
parler to talk, to speak
penser (à) to think (about)
petit, petite little, small
porter to carry, to wear
portugais, portugaise Portuguese
pour for
prêter to lend, to loan
Que veut dire--? What does--
    mean?
quitter to leave
regarder to look at, to watch
rester to stay, to remain
rose pink
rouge red
russe Russian
suédois, suédoise Swedish
suisse Swiss
téléphoner (à) to call
le train train
travailler to work
trouver to find
vert, verte green
les vêtements (mpl) clothes
vieux, vieille old
visiter to visit (a place)
voyager to travel

Structures

Possessive adjectives

Irregular plurals of nouns and adjectives (in **-s, -x, -z; -au, -eau, -eu**)

Present indicative of **-ir** verbs (class I - **finir**; class II - **sortir**)

Cardinal numbers 11 to 20

Objectives

To indicate possession using possessive adjectives

To form irregular plurals of certain nouns and adjectives

To form and use correctly the present indicative of two classes of verbs ending in **-ir**

To recognize and use the cardinal numbers 11 to 20

Rationale

Situation

David essaie son français introduces students to French "sign language," i.e., how to read and understand signs (based on verb forms and derivatives), which one will encounter in everyday situations in France.

Grammaire

Refining the expression of possession, students are introduced to French possessive adjectives to avoid repetition of the structures noun + **de** + noun and **être à**. This point of grammar poses great problems for learners because of the phenomenon of adjective agreement. Certain nouns and adjectives have irregular plural forms that can be categorized according to the ending of the noun or adjective in question. Second conjugation (**-ir**) verbs are presented in two classes, each of which exhibits a consistent pattern of formation in the present indicative. The cardinal numbers 11-20 are introduced. All subsequent counting is based on the numbers 1-20.

Strategies

Situation

All instructional signs are based on verbs and derivative forms:
   a. nouns derived from verbs
   b. past participles
   c. infinitives
   d. imperatives

Students are introduced to verb forms and can realize the variety of usage of such forms through reading signs before formal study of such features is undertaken.

Point out that travelers encounter signs immediately upon arrival in any location and must understand them in order to get along.

Also point out the problem of understanding numbers as they are spoken.

Grammaire

Possessive adjectives may pose problems for learners:

   a. Possessive forms vary according to the gender and number of the item(s) possessed.

   b. No distinction is made in the third person singular between his/her/its.

   c. Certain variant forms in the singular are used, determined by the form of the following noun.

   d. Possessive adjectives must be repeated in a series.

   e. Third person singular and plural forms are often confused.

Activities may be carried out using articles belonging to class members and a questioning technique:

   C'est le livre de Steve?

   Oui, c'est son livre. Non, ce n'est pas son livre.

English, like French, has many irregular forms for the plurals of nouns: mouse/mice, woman/women, deer/deer, etc. Pointing out this similarity makes French a bit less awesome. Adjectives, on the other hand, do not vary in form in English. The basic patterns for nouns are applicable in most cases for adjectives, thereby making the learning task less complex.

Avoid bringing in other exceptions to plural formation at this stage, since many other high frequency adjective and noun forms will be studied in subsequent chapters.

Care must be taken in the introduction of both classes of -ir verbs to avoid initial confusion in forms. Adequate drilling must occur for each class before combining them. Patterns for each class should be clearly spelled out. All in all, there are six basic class II -ir verbs (including **sentir:** to feel, to smell).

Point out the consistent pattern of all plural verb endings (except in the most highly irregular verbs): **-ons, -ez, -ent.** Class I -ir verbs include an **-iss-** infix in the plural; class II verbs do not. Recognition of such a feature simplifies learning.

As with the numbers 0-10, the numbers 11-20 should not be taught and drilled in sequence but in random order to insure adequate learning and ready usage. Concentrate on pronunciation and the distinction between similar pairs: **deux/douze, six/seize.**

Point out that the French counting system in higher numbers is based on twenty (a remnant of a Celtic influence). This is not true in Belgium and Switzerland where the system is based on ten.

Testing

Listening comprehension activities based on
  possessive adjectives
    1. Who is the possessor?
    2. How many things are possessed?
    3. Which thing(s) is (are) possessed?
  singular/plural of nouns and adjectives
  spot dictation (in which all forms of any item--verbs, adjectives,
    nouns, etc.--are omitted and must be filled in in a printed text with
    blanks) using
    1. -ir verbs
    2. possessive adjectives
    3. singular/plural forms of nouns and adjectives
  number perception
    1. Circle the number you hear.
    2. Write the arabic numerals for the numbers heard.
    3. Fill in a chart with the numbers heard.

Fill-in-the-blanks with
  possessive adjectives
  the correct forms of -ir verbs in the present indicative

Rewriting sentences seeded with irregular nouns and adjectives in the plural

Additional materials

D.L. Ellis and M.R. Pearce. French Sign Language. Skokie, IL: National Textbook Company (No. 1880-2)

Signs of the Times, New York: Gessler Publishing Company (No. 4520)

Signposts-France, New York: Gessler Publishing company (No. 4459)

Photos of signs with handwritten numbers for prices

Catalogues (Trois Suisses, Simpsons-Sears (Canada), La Redoute,
Manufrance, etc.) (These are excellent source books.)

Vocabulary

le blazer	blazer
le blouson	jacket
le caleçon	(under)shorts
le costume	suit
la cravate	tie
le fond de robe	slip
les gants (mpl)	gloves
le gilet	undershirt; vest
la jupe	skirt
le jupon	half-slip
le maillot (de bain)	bathing suit
la robe	dress
la sandale	sandal
sentir	to smell, to feel
le short	shorts
le slip	briefs
les sous-vêtements (mpl)	underwear
le soutien-gorge	bra
les trainings (mpl)	tennis shoes; jogging shoes
la veste	sport coat

Mots en action

l'anorak (m) ski jacket
l'appareil (m) camera
après after
aussi too, also
le bateau boat
le bras arm
le cadeau gift
la ceinture belt
le chapeau hat
la chaussette sock
la chemise shirt
le chemisier blouse
le cheveux (mpl) hair
choisir to choose
le choix choice
le contraire opposite
le corps body
le cours class, course

le couteau knife
déranger to bother, to disturb
dormir to sleep
le drapeau flag
l'eau (f) water
l'enfant (m,f) child
fatigué(e) tired
faux, fausse false
le feu fire
le fils son
finir to finish
frapper to hit, to knock
fumer to smoke
le gâteau cake
les gens (mpl) people
l'heure (f) hour
heureux, heureuse happy
le jeu game

le lieu place
malheureux, malheureuse unhappy
le manteau coat
le matin morning
mentir to lie
moi me
le mois month
le morceau piece
le neveu nephew
le nez nose
obéir (à) to obey
l'oiseau (m) bird
le panneau sign
le pantalon pants
paresseux, paresseuse lazy
parfois sometimes
partir (de) to leave; to depart from

le père father
la photo(graphie) photo(graph)
pourquoi why
le prix price, prize
le pull(-over) sweater
punir to punish
remplir to fill
le repas meal
réussir (à) to succeed; to pass
roux, rousse redheaded
servir to serve
sortir (de) to leave; to go out of
le soulier shoe
le tableau picture
te you
très very
le voyage trip

Chapitre Cinq

Structures

Some uses of the definite article (with nouns in a generic or general sense; with specific, identified nouns)

The partitive article (general use; reduced to **de** after negatives (except **être),** before preceding plural adjectives, following adverbs or nouns of quantity)

Irregular plurals of nouns and adjectives (continued) (in **-al, -ail**)

Vouloir (to want): present indicative (+ noun or infinitive; conditional forms for politeness)

Objectives

To use the definite article correctly in both general and specific senses

To form and use the partitive article

To reduce the partitive article to **de** in appropriate circumstances

To form the plural of nouns and adjectives ending in **-al, -ail**

To conjugate and use the present indicative of **vouloir**

To use certain conditional forms of **vouloir** for politeness

Rationale

Situation

Au Restaurant Négroni à Québec introduces students to a Canadian restaurant in Quebec. The bilingual menu reinforces the meanings of names of certain dishes. Some basic terminology for ordering is presented.

Grammaire

The use of the definite article in the specific sense closely parallels English usage. However, use of this article in the generic or general sense is quite different from English and should be stressed. The partitive article per se does not exist in English except with "some" or "any," which are quite frequently omitted. The partitive is peculiar to French (and Italian) and is necessary for accurate communication. Reduction of the partitive and indefinite plural articles to **de** is occasioned by three specific conditions. Additional irregular plural forms of nouns and adjectives ending in **-al** and **-ail** are presented. **Vouloir,** a high-frequency verb, is presented in the present indicative and in selected forms of the conditional.

Strategies

Situation

Using menus from various French restaurants, point out the names of dishes. Note that often the name of the item is not used but a contrived name for how, where, or by whom the dish is prepared is used instead.

Bilingualism in Canada can be discussed briefly.

The protocol for ordering and paying is illustrated. Point out:
  a. the differences between a **carte** and a **menu**
  b. the meaning of **prix net** and **service compris**
  c. how much to tip
  d. how various wines are served

Eating habits are illustrated in **Lecture II, A table avec les Français.**

Grammaire

The definite article used in a generic or general sense does not exist in English. Point out that nouns, except proper names of people and cities, may never occur unmodified.

Frequently, use of the definite article for generic or general meaning is signaled by certain verbs: **aimer, détester, préférer, adorer,** etc.

Most often "in general" or "all" may be inserted into the sentence without changing the meaning when this use of the definite article is questioned.

The definite article used in the specific sense parallels English usage. Whenever the word "the" is used in English, the definite article (either alone or in contracted form) must be used.

The partitive article equivalents in English, "some/any," are most often omitted in English, thereby causing problems for learners. If "some/any" may be inserted into the French sentence, a form of the partitive article must be used, provided "some" means "more than one/an indefinite, unspecified quantity" and not "a few" **(quelques)** or "no matter what" **(quelconque).**

Certain verbs often indicate the need for the partitive article: **il y a, acheter, manger, vouloir, commander,** etc.

Irregular plurals of nouns and adjectives exist only in the masculine plural form, since the feminine plural simply calls for addition of an **-s** to the feminine singular form in all cases. The change from **-al** and **-ail** to **-aux** is a very clear plural marker.

Vouloir may be followed by a noun (most often introduced by the partitive article) or by an infinitive with no intervening preposition.

The use of the conditional forms with **vouloir** signals a degree of politeness not found with the present indicative. These forms should simply be learned and not discussed at this stage.

Testing

Listening comprehension activities including
  use of the definite article
  partitive article
      1.   affirmative/negative
      2.   quantity words
      3.   full or reduced forms with adjectives
  singular/plural of nouns and adjectives ending in **-al, -ail**
  forms and persons of **vouloir**
  polite/strong use of **vouloir**

Personalized activities and questions based on likes and dislikes; preferences; habits in ordering in a restaurant and in eating, clothing, courses, etc.

Mastery activities using traditional forms of test items

Additional Materials

From ACTFL Materials Center:

  Linda Crawford-Lange. "Comment faire un croque-monsieur"

  Robert J. Headrick, Jr. "Ronald McDonald dit: 'Deuxsteakshachés
  saucespécialesaladefromageoignonsdansuntriplepainrondcouvert
  degrainsdesésames'"

  Jan Carlile. "Vous désirez?"

Life--French Style Series, from National Textbook Company:
  "Drinking in France" (No. 1935-1)
  "Food in France" (No. 1936-2)

Menus from French restaurants worldwide

Packaging containers for French food products

"Bon appétit!" card game. Gessler Publishing Company (No. 4713)

From Gessler Publishing Company:

  "Les Français à table" (No. 4211)
  "Marling Menu-Master for France" (No. 4321)
  "Cuisine en français facile" (No. 4188)
  "La cuisine familiale et pratique" (No. 4464)

Vocabulary

l'agneau (m)	lamb
l'ail (m)	garlic
l'ananas (m)	pineapple
les asperges (fpl)	asparagus
le brocoli	broccoli
le champagne	champagne
le champignon	mushroom
le chou	cabbage
le chou-fleur	cauliflower
la confiture	jam, jelly
le crabe	crab
la crème chantilly	whipped cream
la crevette	shrimp
la fraise	strawberry
le jambon	ham
le jus	juice
la mayonnaise	mayonnaise
le melon	melon
la moutarde	mustard
l'œuf (m)	egg
à la coque	hard-boiled egg
brouillé	scrambled egg
poché	poached egg
sur le plat	fried egg

l'oignon (m)	onion
l'omelette (f)	omelette
le pamplemousse	grapefruit
la pêche	peach
le petit pain	roll
la pizza	pizza
la purée de pommes de terre	mashed potatoes
les spaghetti (mpl)	spaghetti
le yaourt (le yoghurt)	yogurt

Mots en action

assez (de) enough

autant (de) as much, as many

beaucoup (de) much, many, a lot le
beurre butter

bien (des) much, many bien sûr of
   course

la bière beer

le bœuf beef

la boisson drink

la bouteille bottle

le café coffee

canadien, canadienne Canadian

la cerise cherry

le cheval horse

la crème cream

le déjeuner lunch

le dîner dinner

la douzaine dozen

encore (some) more

l'entrecôte (f) sirloin steak

les épinards (mpl) spinach

les frites (fpl) french fries

le fromage cheese

la glace ice cream

le haricot vert green bean

les huîtres (fpl) oysters

le journal newspaper

le kilo(gramme) kilogram

le lait milk

la laitue lettuce

les légumes (mpl) vegetables

libre free (unoccupied)

le litre liter

la livre pound

les moules (fpl) mussels

la nourriture food

l'œuf (m) egg

le pain bread

le paquet pack; package

parce que because

la pâtisserie pastry

le petit déjeuner breakfast

le petit pois green pea

peu (de) little
   un peu de a little

plus (de) more

plusieurs several

la poire pear

le poisson fish

le poivre pepper

la pomme apple

la pomme de terre potato

le porc pork

le poulet chicken

le raisin grapes

le restaurant restaurant

le rosbif roast beef

le saumon salmon

le sel salt

la sole sole

le sorbet sherbet

le souper supper

le sucre sugar

la tarte pie

la tasse cup

le temps time

le thé tea

la tomate tomato

la tranche slice

trop (de) too much, too many

la truite trout

le veau veal

le verre glass

la viande meat

le vin wine

voudrais (from vouloir) would
   like

vouloir to want

Chapitre Six

Structures

The present indicative of **-re** verbs

The definite article with geographical names

Prepositions with names of cities

Prepositions with names of countries

Personal pronouns: direct objects (forms; position)

Aller (to go): present indicative (**aller** + infinitive)

Objectives

To form and use the present indicative of **-re** verbs

To use the definite article with geographical names

To use the correct prepositions (+ definite article where needed) to indicate direction toward or away from a geographical location

To use and position direct object pronouns in sentences

To form and use the present indicative of **aller** to indicate motion toward a location

To use the present indicative of **aller** + infinitive to convey the idea of future time

Rationale

Situation

En Europe introduces students to French names of geographical locations in Europe plus the names of continents and certain larger countries. Knowledge of general geographical locations is of great importance.

Grammaire

Third conjugation (**-re**) verbs comprise the last classified conjugation exhibiting regular patterns. The fact that geographical names in French are classified by gender and exhibit spellings at variance with English causes certain problems for students. Furthermore, the use of prepositions (+ definite article) to indicate direction toward or away from these locations is determined by the gender and number of the geographical name. The use of direct object pronouns reduces the repetitive nature of many utterances. Position and form of these pronouns differ markedly from English and should be stressed. **Aller**, another high-frequency irregular verb, is quite versatile in that it indicates direction toward a location and, as an auxiliary verb, is used with a dependent infinitive to indicate future time. Using this construction, students can now express two of the three prime times of verbs: present and future.

Strategies

Situation

Using a map of the world or of western Europe, students should be drilled on basic geographical facts: the names of various countries in French, the location, the capital cities, and other large cities.

Point out the differences in **temps, fois,** and **heure.**

Point out the interrogative tag **n'est-ce pas** and its use compared with English tags.

Grammaire

Many **-re** verbs, while comprising a small part of the corpus of French verbs, are quite common. Emphasize correct pronunciation of the third persons, singular and plural.

Point out the slight irregularity in **rompre (il rompt).**

Point out
  a. the difference between **entendre** and **écouter**
  b. the obligatory use of **à** with **répondre**
  c. the difference between **rendre visite à** (people) and **visiter** (places).

Make sure students understand that the prepositions (+ definite article where needed) used to indicate direction toward or away from geographical location depend on the gender (and number) of the name of that location.

Genders of the names of many states in the US and the names of most third-world countries are not clearly established. When in doubt with state names, it is safe to say **dans l'état de....** Most state names that end in **-a** or **-ia** in English end in **-e, -ie** in French.

Direct object pronouns are conjunctive, weak pronouns. They must form a portion of the verb core of a sentence and therefore are positioned directly before the verb of which they are the object (except in affirmative imperative constructions, which are discussed later). With negation, object pronouns are positioned immediately after **ne.**

Point out that direct object pronouns may replace both personal and nonpersonal direct object nouns.

Warn students about using English translations to determine object pronoun function. Certain verbs take direct objects in French and objects of prepositions in English. Illustrate this using the mnemonic of RED CAP verbs:

Regarder	to look at
Ecouter	to listen to
Demander	to ask for
Chercher	to look for
Attendre	to wait for
Payer	to pay for

Conversely, certain French verbs take objects of prepositions while the English equivalents take direct objects: **réussir à, téléphoner à, obéir à, entrer dans, avoir besoin de.** Object pronoun function should be determined based on the verb as it is used in French.

Point out that with the construction conjugated verb + infinitive, in almost all cases any objects present belong to the infinitive and are placed before it, since the conjugated verb functions as an auxiliary (modal) verb.

Drill the present indicative of **aller** sufficiently because of its versatility and frequency of occurrence.

Drill pronunciation differences between **aller, vouloir** and **aller, être, avoir.**

Stress the use of **aller** + infinitive for expressing future time since it closely parallels English usage and often replaces the future, especially in conversational French.

Testing

Listening comprehension activities including
   singular/plural of **-re** verbs
   gender and number of direct object pronouns
   direction toward or away from geographical locations
   distinction between **aller/avoir**
   future/present tense of **aller**

Identification of countries and capitals (especially western Europe)

Rewriting sentences with direct object pronoun substitutions

Rewriting sentences from the present indicative to the future with **aller**

Personalized questions on travel; seeded questions calling for answers
using direct object pronouns; future plans

Additional Materials

Map of the world (or of western Europe)

Travel books, pamphlets, brochures (preferably in French)

Travel posters

Vocabulary

l'Algérie (f)	Algeria
la Finlande	Finland
la Hongrie	Hungary
l'Israël	Israel
la Jordanie	Jordan
le Liban	Lebanon
la Libye	Libya
le Maroc	Morocco
la Palestine	Palestine
la Roumanie	Roumania
la Tchécoslovaquie	Czechoslovakia
la Tunisie	Tunisia
la Turquie	Turkey
la Yougoslavie	Yugoslavia

(See map in **Lecture V**, page 302.)

Mots en action

l'Afrique (f) Africa
l'Allemagne (f) Germany
aller to go
l'Amérique (f) du Nord North America
l'Amérique (f) du Sud South America
l'Angleterre (f) England
l'Asie (f) Asia
attendre to wait (for)
l'Australie (f) Australia
l'avion (m) airplane
battre to beat
la Belgique Belgium
le billet ticket
le Brésil Brazil
le bruit noise
Bruxelles Brussels
le Canada Canada
la carte card; map
la Chine China

le Danemark Denmark
défendre to defend; to forbid
descendre to come down; to
    descend; to come downstairs
l'Egypte (f) Egypt
entendre to hear
l'Espagne (f) Spain
les Etats-Unis (mpl) United
    States
l'Europe (f) Europe
la fois time
le frère brother
la Grèce Greece
la Hollande Holland
l'Italie (f) Italy
l'itinéraire (m) itinerary
le Japon Japan
le Mexique Mexico
la montagne mountain
mordre to bite

Moscou Moscow
n'est-ce pas? aren't you?
la **Norvège** Norway
le **pays** country
les **Pays-Bas** (mpl) Holland, Netherlands
perdre to lose
la **Pologne** Poland
le **Portugal** Portugal
rendre to give back; to make
rendre visite à to visit (a person)

rentrer to return; to come home
répondre (à) to answer
rompre to break
la **Russie** Russia
spécial(e) special
la **Suède** Sweden
la **Suisse** Switzerland
sur on
les **vacances** (fpl) vacation
vendre to sell
le **Zaïre** Zaïre

Chapitre Sept

Structures

Personal pronouns: indirect objects

The imperative

The position of object pronouns in the imperative (affirmative and negative)

Irregular feminine forms of adjectives (in **-x, -f, -c**)

Venir (to come): present indicative (similar verbs; **venir de**)

Objectives

To use and position indirect object pronouns in a sentence

To form and use regular and irregular forms of the imperative

To position object pronouns in affirmative and negative imperatives

To form the feminine of adjectives ending in **-x, -f, -c**

To form and use the present indicative of **venir** and verbs following the same pattern

To use **venir de** + infinitive to indicate immediate past

Rationale

Situation

Des coups de téléphone introduces students to how to make both long-distance and local phone calls from the **bureau de poste.**

Grammaire

As with direct object pronouns, the use of indirect object pronouns reduces the repetitive nature of many utterances. All conjunctive object pronouns follow the same rules for position in both affirmative and negative sentences. Both direct and indirect object pronoun forms are identical, except for third person singular and plural forms. Imperatives are basically used for making requests and are relatively simple to master because of the similarity with present indicative verb forms, except for the most common irregular verbs. The position of single object pronouns in affirmative imperative constructions varies from that in other constructions as do certain forms. Most feminine forms of adjectives derived from masculine singular forms ending in consonants other than **-t** or **-d** are irregular but follow a consistent pattern of formation. **Venir** is yet another high frequency irregular verb that indicates motion toward a location and, in the construction **venir de** + infinitive, immediate past time. Several other common verbs follow the same conjugation pattern as **venir**.

Strategies

Situation

French telephone numbers are normally given in pairs of digits, but since Paul has just arrived in France and is not comfortable with numbers, he gives the numbers individually.

Point out that an **annuaire** is often called **un bottin**.

Mention that French pay telephones have a timer in them and that coins deposited will disappear from sight after a certain period of elapsed time, indicating that the call will end shortly if another coin is not deposited.

Grammaire

To make learning easier, stress that all indirect object pronouns have the same form as direct object pronouns except in the third persons singular and plural.

Point out that indirect object pronouns may only be used for substitution with personal object nouns.

No distinction is made between masculine and feminine referents for indirect object pronouns in the third persons singular and plural: **lui** means "to him/her"; **leur** means "to them (men, women, or a group of mixed gender)."

Both direct and indirect object pronouns follow the same rules for position in all situations.

Point out verbs that take indirect objects in French and direct objects in English. Students should determine correct pronoun substitution based on the French verb and not on the English equivalent.

Point out that imperative forms of most verbs are similar to equivalent forms of the present indicative. Note particularly that the **tu** form of the imperative of **-er** verbs (including **aller)** drops the final **-s** (unless followed by **y** or **en).**

Make sure students understand that the first person plural imperative form means "let's" + verb (not "let" = **laisser).**

Emphasize that in affirmative imperative constructions, all object pronouns follow the verb and are attached to it with a hyphen. In negative imperative constructions, object pronouns precede the verb.

Point out the regular pattern of the formation of feminine adjectives derived from masculine singular forms ending in **-x, -f.**

Drill the conjugation of the present indicative of **venir,** since it and many verbs that follow the same pattern are high-frequency verbs. Stress the correct pronunciation of all forms, especially the third persons singular and plural.

Emphasize the meaning of **venir de** + infinitive, which conveys the idea of immediate past: "to have just...." Point out that the idiomatic usage of this construction exists only in the present and imperfect tenses.

Testing

Listening comprehension activities including:
    direct/indirect object pronouns
    imperative/nonimperative sentences
    affirmative/negative imperatives
    masculine/feminine irregular adjectives
    venir/venir de

Rewriting sentences replacing indirect object nouns with corresponding indirect object pronouns

Reacting to sentences using affirmative or negative imperatives (with object pronouns where possible)

Fill-in-the-blanks with the appropriate forms of **venir** and verbs that follow the same pattern

Rewriting sentences using the **venir de** construction

Additional Materials

Quénelle et Tournaire. La France dans votre poche, article on telephones

Sample pages from a French-language phone book

Examples of French signs using imperative forms

Vocabulary

le bottin	telephone directory
le cadran	dial
Ne quittez pas.	Don't hang up. Hold on.
l'opérateur (m), l'opératrice (f)	operator
sécher un cours	to cut a class

Mots en action

accepter to accept
l'adresse (f) address
l'agent (m) de voyages travel agent
allô hello
amoureux, amoureuse in love
l'annuaire (m) telephone directory
appartenir to belong
la boum party
la cabine booth
la chambre (bed)room
le chiffre number, digit
le combiné (telephone) receiver
la communication (phone) call
composer to dial
décrocher to pick up (the receiver)
devenir to become
donner un coup de téléphone à to call, to phone
doux, douce sweet, soft
échouer à to fail
en P.C.V. collect
faux, fausse false
franc, franche frank
grec, grecque Greek
le groupe group
l'indicatif (m) code
interurbain long-distance
jamais ever

lever to raise
la monnaie coins, change
neuf, neuve (brand) new
le nombre number
obtenir to obtain, to get
pardonner (à) to pardon
le passeport passport
passer to take (a test)
poser to ask (a question)
raccrocher to hang up (the receiver)
rater (colloq.) to flunk, to miss
régional(e) area
regretter to be sorry, to regret
les renseignements (mpl) information
ressembler (à) to resemble
revenir to return, to come back
sage good, well-behaved
savoureux, savoureuse tasty
sec, sèche dry
souvent often
sportif, sportive athletic
le, la standardiste operator
le téléphone telephone
tenir to hold
la tonalité dial tone
toujours always
utiliser to use
venir to come

Chapitre Huit

Structures

The position of double object pronouns (normal order; affirmative imperative)

More irregular feminine forms of adjectives (in -l, -on, -ien, -s; -er, -et)

Cardinal numbers 21 to 1 000 000

Prendre (to take): present indicative (other similar verbs)

Objectives

To position double object pronouns in all sentences, including affirmative imperatives

To form irregular feminine adjectives

To recognize and use cardinal numbers beginning with 21

To conjugate and use correctly the present indicative of **prendre** and other verbs belonging to the same family

Rationale

Situation

La nouvelle maison shows students the floor plan of a typical French house and the names for many parts of a house and household furnishings. Most French people live in apartments; therefore buying a house is quite important.

Grammaire

The position of double object pronouns differs radically from that of English in all circumstances except in affirmative imperatives. Therefore, learning the correct position and order of occurrence of object pronouns calls for a basic reordering of thought and continuous practice. The last major groupings of irregular feminine adjectives are presented. Now that basic cardinal numbers have been learned (0-20), the remaining numbers follow a relatively consistent pattern within each grouping of ten. Peculiarities of the French system are now introduced. The irregular verb **prendre** is another high-frequency verb, as are the other verbs in the same family.

Strategies

Situation

Point out the basic differences between typical French and American houses: separate bathroom and toilet; shuttered windows; slate or tile roofs; names of floors; etc.

Students must learn to visualize a French house when they hear or read **maison** (as is true with all vocabulary items). A French **fenêtre** generally has two vertical panels that open in as opposed to an American sash window that is raised or lowered. Screens are generally not used in France.

Grammaire

A relatively simple "rule" for remembering the order of double object pronouns in all sentences except affirmative imperatives is: Place the pronoun beginning with any consonant except **l-** first, then the pronoun beginning with **l-**. If both pronouns begin with **l-**, put them in alphabetical order. For affirmative imperatives, put both pronouns in alphabetical order (or in the English word order).

Remind students that in affirmative imperative constructions, pronouns are moved from their normal pre-verb position and that they must be "attached" to the verb with a hyphen. If **me** or **te** occurs in final position, it must become **moi** or **toi**.

Again a relatively predictable pattern of formation of irregular feminine adjectives is found, but more exceptions begin to appear. Note that with masculine singular adjectives ending in **-er, -et,** the change basically makes the written form correlate with pronunciation; two unaccented **e**'s cannot occur in a row separated by only one consonant. This rule is also seen with spelling-change **-er** verbs. (See **Chapitre Quatorze.**)

Point out that **cent** means "one hundred." Beginning with 70, the French counting system based on 20 is easily seen: 70 = 60 + 10. Eighty **(quatre-vingts)** is the same as Lincoln's famous "four score...." The **-s** disappears from **quatre-vingts** and **cents** (as in **deux cents**) when another number follows. Years may be stated in two ways: 1984=
  a. mille neuf cent quatre-vingt-quatre
  b. dix-neuf cent quatre-vingt-quatre

The former (a) is more common.

In Switzerland and Belgium, the count system is based on 10, with different names given to 70, 80, and 90: **septante, octante/huitante, nonante.**

Again, numbers should not be learned or practiced in sequence but in random order to facilitate ready use and recall.

Drill the present indicative conjugation of **prendre**, stressing correct pronunciation and spelling. Point out **passer un examen** = "to take a test"; **suivre un cours** = "to take a course."

Testing

Listening comprehension activities including

   identification of persons in sentences with double pronoun
      substitution
   recognition of masculine/feminine adjective forms
   recognition of spoken numbers
   persons of **prendre**
   recognition of corrrect verb in **prendre** family

Rewriting sentences substituting double object pronouns for object nouns

Fill-in-the-blanks with correct present indicative forms of verbs in the **prendre** family

Personalized questions using object pronoun substitutions

Additional Materials

Photos and illustrations of typical French houses, apartment buildings, and household objects

Floor plans of French houses and apartments

Catalogues with prices for work with numbers

Classified real estate ads from French newspapers

Vocabulary

le bidet	bidet
la cave	cellar
le chauffe-eau	water heater
la cheminée	fireplace; chimney
le couloir	corridor; hall
la cuisinière	stove
le divan	sofa
l'escalier (m)	stairway; stairs
le fauteuil	armchair
le grenier	attic
l'hypothèque (f)	mortgage
le lit	bed
les meubles (mpl)	furniture
la poubelle	garbage can
le rideau	curtain; drape
le robinet	spigot, faucet
le sofa	sofa
le ventilateur	fan

Mots en action

ancien, ancienne old; former
l'appartement (m) apartment
apprendre to learn
l'ascenseur (m) elevator
la baignoire bathtub
le balcon balcony
bavard(e) talkative
bricoler to putter around
le chauffage heating
cher, chère expensive; dear
complet, complète complete, full
comprendre to understand
la cuisine kitchen
dernier, dernière last
la douche shower
encore yet, still
entier, entière entire, whole
l'entrée (f) entrance hall
épais, épaisse thick
l'étage (m) floor (level)
l'évier (m) sink
le four oven
frais, fraîche fresh, cool
le garage garage
l'immeuble (m) apartment building
inquiet, inquiète upset, bothered
le lavabo wash basin

le lave-vaisselle dishwasher
léger, légère light
la lettre letter
le living(-room) living room
le mur wall
la nuit night
particulier, particulière private (home)
la pièce room
le placard closet
premier, première first
prendre to take
raconter to tell (in detail)
le réfrigérateur (**le frigo**) refrigerator
le rez-de-chaussée ground floor
la salle room
  la salle à manger dining room
  la salle de bains bathroom
  la salle de séjour living room
le sous-sol basement
surprendre to surprise
les toilettes (fpl) toilet
le toit roof
la tuile tile
le volet shutter
les w.-c. toilet, bathroom

Chapitre Neuf

Structures

Time of day (12- and 24-hour systems)

Past participles of regular verbs (including irregular verbs studied thus far)

The passé composé (with **avoir**) (formation; uses; negation; position of object pronouns)

Agreement of the past participle

Faire (to do; to make) (weather expressions; sports; other expressions)

Objectives

To tell time using both the 12- and the 24-hour systems

To form the past participles of regular and selected irregular verbs

To use past participles as adjectives

To form and use appropriately the passé composé of verbs with **avoir** as auxiliary in both affirmative and negative, declarative and interrogative sentences

To make past participle agreement where appropriate

To conjugate and use correctly the present indicative and passé composé of **faire**

Rationale

Situation

"Dallas" en France introduces students to expressions of time, including present and past tenses, and to the current international status and influence of American television. It is interesting to note that France has only three different channels.

Grammaire

Telling time in French differs from English since both the 12- and 24-hour systems are consistently used and since each system calls for a totally different method of stating time. Students are introduced to many different expressions of time. Correct past participle formation is important to the use of the participles as adjectives and as components of compound tenses. The passé composé is the third tense vital for functional, basic expression of time (past, the present indicative, and the future using **aller** + infinitive). Implications of meaning of the passé composé must be understood now before study of the imperfect tense is undertaken. Past participle agreement, primarily a feature of the written language, should be understood and used correctly in formal writing. It is also often an aid in reading comprehension. The irregular verb **faire** is yet another high-frequency verb that must be mastered early since it forms the core of many everyday expressions.

Strategies

Situation

Using television schedules, much work can be done on drilling time-- hour of day; days; past, present, and future times; repetition of days; etc.

Such schedules also provide much cultural information concerning TV viewing in France: types of programs, schedules, news, advertisements, etc.

Point out that advertisements and commercials are not interspersed throughout a program but appear at fixed times in a block.

Many movie write-ups are good springboards for narrative use of the passé composé.

Grammaire

Have students tell time (including AM and PM when necessary) using a clock, class schedules, train and plane schedules, television schedules, etc.

Point out that on the 24-hour system, time is told using sequential numbers from hour to hour with no subtraction and alternate expressions (**quart, demi**).

Point out that written forms of time on the 12-hour system often differ radically from the statement of the same time as it is spoken.

Drill names of months and days of the week in random order to avoid simple memorization. Calendars can be used effectively in this activity.

Point out the difference in meaning of **jour/journée, an/année,** etc. Short forms are generally used with numbers: **deux ans.**

Distinguish carefully among **heure/temps/fois.**

Stress the use of the definite article with names of the days of the week to indicate repeated, habitual action. Point out that "on" is included in this expression.

Remind students that months, days, and seasons are not capitalized in French.

Drill the present indicative of **avoir** since it is the major auxiliary verb.

Work consistently with writing in the passé composé, rewriting from the present tense. Such activities are most effective and most meaningful in connected passages with a clear context rather than in isolated sentences, which normally call for many stated time words and expressions that falsify actual usage.

Stress the implications of meaning of the passé composé.

Do not stress past participle agreement unless there is feminine agreement in a past participle ending in a consonant: **prise, écrite,** etc.

Drill the conjugation of the present indicative of **faire**, stressing **vous faites** and the correct pronunciation of plural forms.

Emphasize **faire** used in expressions of weather and contrast with **avoir** for expressing physical reactions.

Point out that **faire de** + the name of a sport = **jouer à** + the name of a sport.

Point out the various verbal expressions using **faire** + noun, most of which are extremely common.

Testing

Listening comprehension activities including
   recognition of time of day
   past participle/infinitive
   present/passé composé
   discrimination between **faire/aller**

Stating of time of day using clock faces, schedules, etc.

Names of days, months

Rewriting continuous passages of prose (originally written in the present indicative) in the passé composé (Anecdotes and film or TV program résumés are good sources of inspiration.)

Recognition of weather, sports, and general activities using illustrations of expressions with **faire**.

Personalized activities involving passé composé and expressions with **faire**.

Additional Materials

SNCF materials (schedules) for time and geography study

TV schedules for time and cultural information

A clock face with movable hands

Sources for anecdotes for work in the passé composé

Illustrations of weather and sports activities

Vocabulary

l'averse (f)	downpour
le brouillard	fog, mist, haze
le calendrier	calendar

l'éclair (m)	a flash of lightning
les éclairs (mpl)	lightning
le foudre	lightning
l'horaire (m)	schedule; timetable
l'horloge (f)	clock
le lendemain	the next day
la neige	snow
la pendule	(pendulum) clock
l'orage (m)	(thunder)storm
la pluie	rain
la prévision	forecast
le réveil-matin	alarm clock
la température	temperature
le tonnerre	thunder

Mots en action

l'achat (m) purchase
l'an (m) year
l'année (f) year
l'après-midi (m) afternoon
l'arrivée (f) arrival
l'auto-stop (m) hitchhiking
bientôt soon
causer to cause
la chaîne channel
les courses (fpl) errands
couvert cloudy
la cuisine cooking
demain tomorrow
le départ departure
d'habitude usually
l'émission (f) broadcast
entendre dire to hear (it said that)
faire to do; to make; to play
le football soccer
  le football américain football
le footing hiking
frais (fraîche) chilly
froid(e) cold
l'heure (f) (clock) time; hour
hier yesterday
Il gèle. It's freezing.

Il grêle. It's hailing.
Il neige. It's snowing.
Il pleut. It's raining.
jouer to play
  jouer à to play (sport)
  jouer de to play (instrument)
le jour day
la journée day
(son) mieux best
la montre watch
la natation swimming
passé(e) last
la planche à voile windsurfing
la promenade walk
quand when
quelque chose something
la semaine week
le soir evening
la soirée evening
le soleil sun
le temps weather; time
le tennis tennis
la vaisselle dishes
la valise suitcase
  faire la valise to pack
le vent wind

Chapitre Dix

Structures

Verbs conjugated with **être** in the passé composé (excluding reflexive verbs)

Position of adjectives (continued) (adjectives with two meanings depending on position)

Expressions with **avoir**

Dire (to say), **écrire** (to write), **lire** (to read)

Objectives

To form and use appropriately the passé composé of verbs using **être** as auxiliary

To use certain normally intransitive verbs as transitive verbs with **avoir** as auxiliary

To position adjectives correctly to show true meaning intended

To use expressions with **avoir** readily, especially in speaking of physical feelings

To conjugate and use correctly the irregular verbs **dire, écrire, lire** in the present indicative and passé composé

Rationale

Situation

Comment ça va? introduces students to vocabulary and structures necessary to talk about health and physical feelings. Nothing is more frightening than being ill in a country in whose language one is not very conversant. Also introduced is the preposition **chez.**

Grammaire

The fact that French has two auxiliary verbs while English has only one can be quite problematic for many students. There are relatively few verbs that take **être** as the auxiliary, but most of them are quite common. Furthermore, obligatory past participle agreement is seen with this group of verbs. While English frequently resorts to tone of voice to indicate figurative and literal meanings of adjectives, French uses different positions--pre- or post-noun. Many expressions with **avoir** deal with physical well-being and health. Potential confusion occurs since English most often uses "to be" while French uses **avoir** or **faire** and rarely **être.** The common irregular verbs **dire, écrire, lire** follow similar patterns in the conjugation of the present indicative--differences are noted in the plural forms and in past participle formation.

Strategies

Situation

Point out the use of **chez** as a preposition, as well as the difference between **en** and **dans** + time expressions.

Note the use of the passé composé with **être.**

Here and in drilling expressions with **avoir,** parts of the body can easily be included.

Grammaire

Point out variable past participle agreement with **nous/vous.**

Do not use the category "intransitive verbs of motion" for signaling which verbs are conjugated with **être**—there are too many exceptions. You might use pairing, the "House of **être**" (see **Révision IV,** exercice 4), or a mnemonic such as DR & MRS VANDERTRAMP (see **Cahier d'exercices,** Chapitre Dix, exercice IIA).

Point out the transitive use of **descendre, monter, sortir** and the necessary use of **avoir** as the auxiliary verb.

Point out the obligatory use of prepositions of location with **aller, entrer, partir, sortir.**

Although French uses two different auxiliary verbs, they both convey the idea of the single English auxiliary "to have."

Certain adjectives convey a literal meaning when they follow nouns, while in a pre-noun position they assume a figurative meaning. English uses the same adjective in the same fixed position coupled with tone of voice to distinguish between figurative and literal meanings:

```
old     = former/in age
dear    = beloved/expensive
last    = immediately preceding/final
poor    = penniless/to be pitied
proper  = clean/one's own
certain = sure/a particular
etc.
```

In many cases with expressions using **avoir, avoir** is equivalent to the English "to be." Contrast this with **faire** and expressions of weather.

Point out the double meaning of **doigt:** finger/toe. Also mention the French preoccupation with **le foie.**

Point out forms of **dire, écrire, lire** that vary from the pattern of present indicative conjugation: **vous dites.** Only three verbs do not have **-ez** as an ending in the **vous** form of present indicative: **être, faire, dire.** Point out the past participle of **lire = lu.** With **dire/écrire,** feminine past participle agreement can be heard.

Testing

Listening comprehension activities including
    distinction between present indicative forms of **dire, écrire, lire**
    être/avoir as auxiliary verbs
    meaning of adjectives in various positions

Fill-in-the-blanks with appropriate forms of **dire, écrire, lire**

Rewriting sentences replacing clues with expressions using **avoir**

Rewriting sentences in the present indicative in the passé composé

Rewriting verbs in a connected passage in the passé composé using either **être** or **avoir** as auxiliaries; **dire, écrire, lire;** expressions with **avoir**

Additional materials

Figure of a man or woman for identification of parts of the body

French medicine containers

Vocabulary

l'allergie (f)	allergy
l'annulaire (m)	ring finger
la blessure	wound, injury
la capsule	capsule
la carie	cavity
se casser	to break
les cils (mpl)	eyelashes
le comprimé	tablet
la crise cardiaque	heart attack
le dentier	denture
la diarrhée	diarrhea
éternuer	to sneeze
la fesse	buttock
se fouler	to sprain
la gorge	throat
guérir	to cure
les honoraires (fpl)	(doctor's) fees
l'index (m)	index finger
la joue	cheek
la lèvre	lip
supérieure	upper
inférieure	lower
la maladie	illness
le médicament	medicine
le menton	chin
le mollet	calf (of leg)
se moucher	to blow one's nose
le nombril	navel
les oreillons (mpl)	mumps
panser	to dress (a wound)
le petit doigt	little finger
la pilule	pill
la piqûre	shot, injection
le plombage	filling
le pouce	thumb

le rhume	bad cold
la rougeole	measles
la rubéole	German measles
la salle d'urgence (f)	emergency room
le sang	blood
le sein	breast
souffrir (de)	to suffer (from)
les sourcils (mpl)	eyebrows
tousser	to cough
la toux	cough

Mots en action

l'aspirine (f)	aspirin
avoir ____ ans	to be ____ years old
avoir besoin en	to need
avoir chaud	to be warm or hot
avoir envie de	to feel like
avoir faim	to be hungry
avoir froid	to be cold
avoir honte	to be ashamed
avoir l'air	to seem, to look
avoir lieu	to take place
avoir mal à ____	to have a(n) ____ ache
avoir peur de	to be afraid of
avoir raison	to be right
avoir rendez-vous avec	to have an appointment or date with
avoir soif	to be thirsty
avoir sommeil	to be sleepy
avoir tort	to be wrong
la bouche	mouth
le bras	arm
brave	good; brave
le cabinet	(doctor's) office
certain(e)	certain; sure
le cheville	ankle
chez	at the home or place of business of
le cœur	heart
le cou	neck
le coude	elbow
la cuisse	thigh
la dent	tooth
dire	to say
le doigt	finger; toe
le dos	back
écrire	to write
enrhumé(e)	to have a bad cold
l'épaule (m)	shoulder
l'estomac (m)	stomach
la fièvre	fever
le foie	liver
le genou	knee
la grippe	flu
la jambe	leg
la langue	tongue

lire	to read
le lit	bed
la main	hand
le médecin	doctor
même	same; very
mourir	to die
naître	to be born
l'œil (m), les yeux (mpl)	eye, eyes
l'ordonnance (f)	prescription
l'oreille (f)	ear
pâle	pale
pendant	during, while, for
le pied	foot
le poignet	wrist
la poitrine	chest
propre	own; clean
le symptôme	symptom
la température	temperature
la tête	head
tomber	to fall
le ventre	abdomen

Chapitre Onze

Structures

Disjunctive personal pronouns (after prepositions; for emphasis; in comparisons when the verb is not expressed; to stress subject or object; in compound subjects or objects; after être à)

The imperfect tense

The imperfect: incomplete past actions

The imperfect: repeated past actions

The imperfect: past conditions

Imperfect versus passé composé

Savoir (to know how)

Objectives

To use disjunctive pronouns correctly

To form the imperfect tense

To use the imperfect tense appropriately

To use the imperfect tense and passé composé discriminately and
appropriately

To conjugate and use correctly the present indicative, passé composé,
and imperfect forms of **savoir**

Rationale

Situation

Comment voyager dans le métro instructs students in the basics of
riding the **métro** in Paris and affords the opportunity for detailed
study of the city (see **Lecture VIII**). This **Situation** introduces the
active use of the passé composé and the imperfect tenses in context.

Grammaire

In contrast to English, which uses voice emphasis for stressing words,
French uses stylistic and structural devices for the same effect.
Disjunctive pronouns may be used alone and as objects of prepositions.
The imperfect tense in French has no counterpart in English, and since
it refers to the same time period as the passé composé but presents a
different perspective in viewing past time, its use presents a major
problem for English-speaking students. The irregular verb **savoir** can
present difficulties for speakers of English due to the dual
interpretations of "to know": factual knowledge versus familiarity
with or acquaintance with.

Strategies

Situation

The Parisian **métro** is one of the oldest and most efficient underground
systems of public transportation. Since most stations do not have the
names of the monuments above ground, a traveler needs to know the
basic layout of the city and the location of major points of interest
before undertaking a trip through Paris.

Note the use of the passé composé and imperfect tenses in context in a
continuous passage—along with the present indicative.

Point out the use of the tag question **hein?** = n'est-ce pas?

Grammaire

Disjunctive personal pronouns are also commonly called emphatic
pronouns. Opposed to conjunctive personal pronouns (subject, direct
object, indirect object), which cannot stand alone, appear in a
position of emphasis in a sentence, or be separated from a verb,
disjunctive pronouns must be used under these circumstances.

Point out the use of disjunctive pronouns with compound subjects and
objects.

Understanding the implications of the use of the imperfect tense is crucial to sensing the subtle nuances of expressions of concepts of past time. The imperfect must not be taught based on English translation equivalents but on specific meanings and implications inherent in the French forms.

It is strongly recommended to read the article by R.M. Terry, "Concepts of Pastness: The passé composé and the imperfect," Foreign Language Annals, Vol. 14, No. 2 (April 1981), 105-110, for a full discussion of methods for teaching the contrast between the passé composé and imperfect.

The contrast between tenses must be taught in context in continuous passages devoid of most "crutch" structures (specific expressions of time); students must rely on the relationships between the perspectives in viewing the actions in question (see Additional Materials).

Note the interplay between the passé composé and imperfect tenses in this diagram of the passage on page 214 in the text:

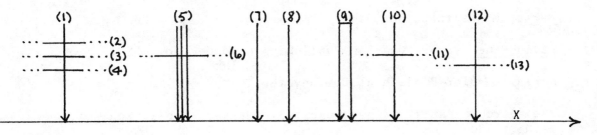

The use of time lines is most effective in presenting visual reinforcement of a highly abstract concept of time relationships.

Emphasize the fact that **savoir** is used to indicate acquired knowledge, factual information. **Savoir** is often followed by a clause introduced with **que.** **Savoir** also means "to know how to" or "can" in the sence of knowing how to do something and not physical ability (**pouvoir**).

When used in the passé composé, **savoir** means "learned, found out," i.e., it indicates the onset of knowledge. **Savoir,** however, occurs most commonly in the imperfect tense—having knowledge.

Testing

Listening comprehension activities including
    referents of disjunctive pronouns
    emphatic/nonemphatic sentences
    imperfect/present indicative
    imperfect/passé composé
    savoir/avoir distinction

Fill-in-the-blanks with appropriate forms of the present indicative of **savoir**

Rewriting a passage in the passé composé and imperfect

Fill-in-the-blanks with appropriate disjunctive pronouns

Additional Materials

Robert M. Terry. "Let Cinderella and Luke Skywalker Help You Teach the Passé composé and Imperfect." ACTFL Materials Center

Métro map and map of Paris (see "Paris Monumental"). Gessler Publishing Company (No. 4526)

Quénelle et Tournaire. La France dans votre poche, sections on the métro

Jan Carlile. "Riding the Métro." ACTFL Materials Center

Paris, Michelin Green Guide

Riding the métro. Gessler Publishing company (No. 4282)

Paris. Gessler Publishing Company (No. 428)7

"Le métro de Paris" (jigsaw puzzle). Gessler Publishing Company (No. 4730)

"Paris métro" (game), Gessler Publishing Company (No. 4764)

Vocabulary

aîné(e)	older, oldest
bondé(e)	crammed, packed
cadet(te)	younger, youngest
le cousin germain	first cousin
l'escalier roulant	escalator
la foule	crowd
la marraine	godmother
oblitérer	to obliterate, to cancel (a ticket)
le parrain	godfather
la rame	métro train
R.A.T.P. (Régie autonome de transports parisiens)	management of métro and bus lines in paris
le tourniquet	turnstile
le trajet	trip (by métro, bus)
le trottoir roulant	moving sidewalk

Mots en action

autrefois	formerly
le carnet (de tickets)	book (of tickets)
changer de	to change
la correspondance	connection
le cousin, la cousine	cousin
se débrouiller	to manage; to get along
la famille	family
la fille	daughter
la grand-mère	grandmother
le grand-parent	grandparent
le grand-père	grandfather
hein?	huh?
la ligne	line
la mère	mother
la nièce	niece
l'oncle (m)	uncle
les parents (mpl)	parents; relatives
puisque	since
le quai	platform
savoir	to know (how)
la station	station (métro, bus, taxi)
la tante	aunt
tous les jours	every day
tout à coup	all of a sudden

Chapitre Douze

Structures

Reflexive verbs

Relexive verbs in the passé composé

Formation of adverbs

Position of adverbs

Depuis + present tense

Objectives

To conjugate and use correctly reflexive verbs in the tenses studied thus far

To form adverbs from adjectives

To position adverbs correctly in sentences

To use the present indicative with **depuis** and synonymous expressions

-57-

Rationale

Situation

Savez-vous être français? An integral component of language is the use of kinesics (body language and gestures), most frequently coupled with words. Different languages use different gestures. To Americans, most foreigners seem to talk with their hands. Therefore, students should be exposed to this facet of language (see **Pour parler** on page 240.

Grammaire

Reflexive verbs pose certain problems for language learners: the correlation of the reflexive pronoun with the subject pronoun and verb form, the position of the reflexive pronoun, the formation of the passé composé and concomitant past participle agreement, and certain subtleties in meaning. Adverbs are grammatical elements that add information to sentences: time, reason, cause, quantity, place, manner. Although adverbs are very mobile elements in a sentence, usage has established "normal" positions for placement. French uses certain idiomatic constructions for indicating subtle nuances of time: action beginning at a certain point in the past and continuing to the present.

Strategies

Situation

It is important to point out that body language and gestures aid significantly in complementing adequate communication. If not, why is it so difficult to understand spoken language on the telephone and radio (and in the language laboratory) when the speaker cannot be seen? Lip reading, facial and body gestures, and sounds fill gaps of misunderstanding or frequently replace words. The nationalities of many people can be identified by how they talk, walk, dress, and carry themselves.

These cultural tidbits greatly enhance understanding and communication and give a certain flair to the language of even the beginning language learner.

Both the teacher and students should use gestures and body language consistently when using French.

Illustrate the need for and use of gestures by asking students to define **une spirale** in French.

Point out when and with whom one shakes hands and to whom **on fait la bise.**

Grammaire

English does not have reflexive pronouns per se, so the concept itself is foreign to students. Point out that the reflexive pronoun must be in the same person as the subject (either stated or understood) of the verb.

Reflexive verbs are also called <u>pronominal</u> verbs. One of the major functions of these verbs is reflexive, along with reciprocal verbs and those that are inherently reflexive. Explain that:

In reflexive use, the pronoun is either a direct or an indirect object and the action of the verb is carried out by the subject on the subject.

In reciprocal use, the verb is by nature plural since at least two people are necessary to reciprocate. The pronoun may again function as a direct or indirect object. Reciprocal verbs convey the meaning of "(to) each other."

In inherently reflexive verbs, the reflexive pronoun most frequently cannot be translated into English. Reflexive pronouns in inherently reflexive verbs are considered to function as direct objects.

Point out that when a reflexive verb is used dependently (preceded by a conjugated verb), the reflexive pronoun must be in the correct form as determined by the subject of the conjugated verb.

In the passé composé, although reflexive verbs are conjugated with **être** as the auxiliary, they follow **avoir** rules for past participle agreement—the past participle agrees when the reflexive pronoun functions as a preceding direct object. Point out that:

If a stated noun direct object follows the verb, the past participle will not agree.

When the reflexive pronoun = "to/for oneself" or "to each other," there is no agreement.

In all other cases the past participle will agree.

Emphasize that when a reflexive verb is used to indicate an action carried out on a part of the body, a definite article is used to indicate possession instead of a possessive adjective.

While discussing adverbs, stress the distinction between **bon/bien** and **mauvais/mal.**

Mention that French **-ment** is equivalent to the English adverb ending **-ly.**

Emphasize that certain adverbs do not end in **-ment: beaucoup, bien, trop, vite,** etc.

In simple tenses, most adverbs normally follow the verb. In compound tenses, most short adverbs (i.e., those not ending in **-ment**) usually follow the auxiliary verb; adverbs of time and longer adverbs (ending in **-ment**) usually follow the past participle.

The idiomatic use of the present with **depuis** to indicate that an action began in the past and is still going on is difficult to grasp. Time lines may help illustrate the concept.

Point out that with hours, it is advisable to use **depuis** to indicate "since...o'clock" and an alternate construction **(il y a/voilà, ça fait)** to indicate "for ... hours," due to the ambiguity of **depuis deux heures.**

Point out that if **il y a** + a time expression occurs at the end of a sentence or clause, it means "ago."

Testing

Listening comprehension activities including
    adverb/adjective distinction
    reflexive/nonreflexive verbs
    present/passé composé and present/imperfect of reflexive verbs
    idiomatic/non-idiomatic uses of the present and imperfect of verbs,
    especially with **il y a, voilà,** and **ça fait**

Inserting adverbs into sentences in the correct position

Transformation of adjectives to adverbs

Adverbial equivalents of adjectives

Personalized questions concerning daily routines using reflexive verbs, adverbs, and the idiomatic present tense with **depuis**

Additional Materials

Laurence Wylie and Rick Stafford. <u>Beaux Gestes: A Guide to French Body Talk.</u> Cambridge, MA: The Undergraduate Press, 1977

Illustrations of actions of reflexive verbs

Vocabulary

se faire la bise	to kiss on the cheek
Je m'en fiche.	I don't give a darn.
Je m'en fous. (vulgar)	I don't give a damn.
le shake-hand	handshake
vachement (colloquial)	very (=**très**)

Mots en action

s'amuser	to have a good time
s'appeler	to be called, to be named
s'arrêter	to stop
se baigner	to bathe
bientôt	soon
se brosser	to brush
se coucher	to go to bed
couramment	fluently
d'abord	at first
de bonne heure	early
se demander	to wonder
se dépêcher	to hurry (up)
depuis	since, for
s'en aller	to leave
encore	again, still, yet
s'endormir	to fall asleep
se fâcher	to get angry
se faire mal à ____	to hurt one's ____
s'habiller	to get dressed
s'intéresser à	to be interested in
jamais	ever, never
se laver	to wash, to bathe
se lever	to get up
longtemps	for a long time
se maquiller	to put on makeup
se marier (avec)	to get married
se mettre à	to begin to
se moquer de	to make fun of
s'occuper de	to be busy with
parfait(e)	perfect
se peigner	to comb
quelquefois	sometimes
quotidien(ne)	daily
se rappeler	to remember; to recall
se raser	to shave
rencontrer	to meet (to bump into)
se reposer	to rest
se réveiller	to wake up
se sécher	to dry
se sentir	to feel
se serrer	to shake (hands)
se souvenir de	to remember
tard	late
tout à l'heure	in a little while
tout de suite	immediately
se tromper de	to be mistaken about
vraiment	really

Chapitre Treize

Structures

Interrogative adverbs with **est-ce que**
Interrogative adverbs with inversion (simple and complex)
The pronoun **y**
The pronoun **en**
The pronouns **y** and **en** (continued)
The relative pronoun **qui**
The relative pronoun **que**
Voir (to see)

Objectives

To form and ask appropriate questions with interrogative adverbs to elicit the information sought

To use **y** correctly as an adverbial and pronominal substitute

To use **en** correctly as an adverbial and pronominal substitute

To use the relative pronoun **qui** appropriately in complex sentences

To use the relative pronoun **que** appropriately in complex sentences

To conjugate and use **voir** in the various tenses studied thus far

Rationale

Situation

Most travelers in Europe use the efficient rail system. **Le train pour Amsterdam** introduces students to key vocabulary items and procedures involved in train travel.

Grammaire

Interrogative adverbs are commonly used in information gathering. Appropriate selection of the interrogative adverb and the structure of the question are vital for effective information-seeking. Adverbial questions using **est-ce que** are of relatively low frequency of use by native speakers. **Y** and **en** are highly unusual pronominal/adverbial substitutes. The use of relative pronouns in combining sentences to avoid repetition is difficult for speakers of English due to (1) the frequent omission of such pronouns in English and (2) the low frequency of such complex sentences in everyday oral communication. **Voir** is a commonly used irregular verb.

Strategies

Situation

Point out classes on a train and when a **supplément** is paid.

Many students will travel with a Eurail Pass, which must be bought before departing the US and is used in western Europe (excluding Great Britain). Contact a travel agent for information.

Grammaire

Mention that in everyday conversation, adverbial questions frequently end with the interrogative adverb and have normal word order: **Tu pars quand?**

Note that in all adverbial questions (except those with **pourquoi**), simple inversion minus the hyphen may occur with noun subjects provided the verb is in a simple tense and the subject noun is the last word.

Y may be substituted for any preposition of location + the name of the location, except the preposition **de.** In most instances, **y** replaces **à** or **dans.** **Y** is considered a vowel and elision occurs before it.

Y as a pronoun substitutes only for nonpersonal objects of **à.** Personal objects of **à** are replaced with (a) indirect object pronouns or (b) in the case of certain verbs, **à** + disjunctive pronouns: **faire attention à, penser à, s'intéresser à.**

En as an adverbial substitute replaces the preposition **de** + the name of the location.

En as a pronoun substitute is generally used with nonpersonal nouns, but may be used with personal nouns as nonspecific references. **En** also substitutes for quantified nouns (partitive, adverbs or nouns of quantity, numbers) when the quantity word is the last word in the clause after substitution. When the number is **un/une, en** may be omitted in negative sentences: **J'en ai un(e),** but **Je n'en ai pas.**

Point out verbs in French that call for **de** + noun object: **avoir besoin de, avoir peur de, se souvenir de, se passer de, se servir de, s'occuper de, se moquer de, se tromper de.**

Point out that in affirmative imperatives (**tu** form), the final **-s** is restored when the verb is followed by **y** or **en.**

Note that **y** precedes **en** in position (the "Donkey rule," as in **il y en a),** and both come after all other object pronouns.

Correct relative pronoun selection is determined by the function of the pronoun (or word to be replaced) in the relative clause.

The relative pronoun must always directly follow the antecedent--the word to which it refers. Although invariable in form, relative pronouns "assume" the gender and number of the antecedent. This is important for adjective and past participle agreement.

The -i of **qui** is never dropped, while the -e of **que** is elided before a following vowel or mute **h**.

Point out that the difference in pronunciation between **nous voyons/nous voyions** and **vous voyez/vous voyiez** is quite subtle and that most often context will determine correct meaning. **Croire** (Chapitre 17) is conjugated exactly like **voir**. Point out the difference in meaning between **voir** and **regarder**.

Testing

Listening comprehension activities including
    qui/que as relative pronouns
    y/en
    adverbial/nonadverbial questions
    tenses and persons of **voir**

Recombination of sentences replacing the repeated element with the appropriate relative pronoun

Rewriting sentences replacing objects with pronoun substitutes: **y, en;** indirect objects or **y;** indirect objects, **y** or preposition + disjunctive pronoun

Fill-in-the-blank with the appropriate form and tense of **voir**

Personalized activities calling for **y, en,** relative pronouns

Interview format with all questions missing (See sample in introduction.)

Additional Materials

Realia from SNCF concerning trains: schedules, photos, tickets, etc.

Quénelle et Tournaire. <u>La France dans votre poche</u>, section on trains

"Voyage en France" (game), Gessler Publishing Company (No. 4746)

Vocabulary

le coin	corner
enregistrer	to check (baggage)
le fumeur	smoker
le gril-express	fast food service
le libre-service	self-service
la malle	trunk

pencher	to lean
prévoir	to foresee
le tarif	price
valable	valid
la vente ambulante	vending
le wagon	(train) car
le wagon-lit	sleeping car, pullman car
le wagon-restaurant	dining car

Mots en action

les bagages (mpl)	luggage, bags
le (billet) aller et retour	round-trip ticket
le (billet) aller simple	one-way ticket
le buffet	snack bar
le chemin de fer	railroad
la consigne	baggage check room
la couchette	berth
l'express (m)	express train (stops at major stations)
le guichet	ticket window
les jeunes gens (mpl)	young men; youth
le kiosque	newsstand
louer	to rent; to reserve
la place	seat
la queue	line
faire la queue	to stand in line
le rapide	express train (no stops)
la salle d'attente	waiting room
la sorte	kind, sort, type
le supplément	supplement
voir	to see
la voiture	(train) car
le voyageur	traveler

Chapitre Quatorze

Structures

The future tense

Uses of the future tense (after **quand, lorsque, dès que, aussitôt que;** in sentences with **si**-clauses; replacement with present indicative or **aller** + infinitive)

Verbs like **payer**

Verbs like **lever**

Verbs like **préférer**

Verbs like **appeler** and **jeter**

Verbs like **commencer** and **manger**

Pouvoir (to be able to, can, may)

Objectives

To form and use the future tense appropriately

To make spelling changes in **-er** verbs

To conjugate and use correctly the irregular verb **pouvoir** in the various
tenses studied thus far

Rationale

Situation

Faisons des achats introduces students to various terms used in
making purchases in French. Few people go to France without making
some purchases--clothes, souvenirs, food, etc.

Grammaire

The use of the future tense in French closely parallels English usage
except after certain adverbs of time. Except for irregular verbs, the
formation of the future tense is standard. Orthographic changes in
-er verbs are based on phonetic principles. These changes correlate
the written form with the spoken form. Most students have been
pronouncing these verbs correctly but have not yet learned the
orthographic forms. **Pouvoir**, a high-frequency irregular verb, has a
conjugation pattern similar to **vouloir**. Meaning distinctions must be
made between **pouvoir** and **savoir**.

Strategies

Situation

Point out the versatility of the word **truc** (and its synonym **machin**) to
make up for vocabulary deficiencies.

Point out size differences between French clothing (and other European
countries) and clothing purchased in the United States. Many sizes
are based on the metric system.

Note that one pays **à la caisse.**

Mention that many well-known American credit cards (Visa, MasterCard, American Express) are accepted in France.

Mention that sales tax is already included in the sale price of an article in France (including food).

Traveler's checks, especially in the currency of the country, may be used for purchases. If the checks are in American dollars, it is advisable to change them at a bank.

Grammaire

The future tense is based on the future stem (the infinitive with regular verbs) + the present indicative of **avoir**: **-ai, -as, -a, -ons, -ez, -ont,** less the **av-** base in the **nous** and **vous** forms. This principle greatly simplifies learning. There are no exceptions.

The future tense must be used in French after **quand, lorsque, dès que, aussitôt que** when futurity is implied, regardless of what is said in English.

In sentences with **si** clauses, the future tense never occurs in the **si** clause (when **si** = "if"). It is most often found in the result clause, but may be replaced by a present tense or an imperative, depending on meaning.

Although a useful, common tense, the future most often can be replaced by **aller** + infinitive. Frequently the present tense can convey the idea of future also. Do not belabor the use of the future tense at this stage, but students should certainly be able to recognize and use it.

Spelling changes in **-er** verbs simply bring written forms in line with pronunciation. As pointed out in the discussion of certain irregular feminine adjective forms, French does not allow two unaccented **e**'s in a row separated by a single consonant; either a grave accent must be added or the consonant doubled. There is no simple device to indicate which change occurs with which specific verb.

Although verbs ending in **-ayer** allow the use of **-y-** or **-i-**, it is simple to regularize the system by discussing this change for all **-yer** verbs.

These spelling changes occur only when the tense/person ending of the verb is silent in the present indicative and present subjunctive. All changes carry through in the future and conditional tenses, except with verbs like **préférer.**

-Cer and **-ger** verbs change only when the **-c-** or **-g-** is followed directly by **-a, -o,** or **-u.**

Pouvoir must be distinguished from **savoir;** the former indicates physical ability, the latter ability as a result of training or instruction.

Pouvoir occurs most commonly in the imperfect tense rather than the passé composé. In the passé composé it indicates "could (and did/did not)." It is used in the conditional tense for politeness.

Testing

Listening comprehension activities including future/present tense, future/past tense(s), **pouvoir/vouloir** discrimination

Fill-in-the-blanks with appropriate forms of the present indicative of spelling change **-er** verbs

Personalized completion of sentences with **si** clauses

Pouvoir/savoir distinctions

Additional Materials

Brochures and catalogues from various boutiques, shops, and department stores

Size conversion charts

Metric tape measure

Packaging from French clothing

Vocabulary

acheter à crédit	to buy on credit
la bijouterie	jewelry store
la confiserie	candy store
la cordonnerie	shoe repair shop
l'épicerie (f)	grocery store
le/la fleuriste	florist
le grand magasin	department store
le joailler	jeweler
la librairie	bookstore
le machin	thing-a-ma-jig, whatcha-ma-callit
la maroquinerie	leather-goods shop
la parfumerie	perfume shop
la pâtisserie	pastry shop
la quincaillerie	hardware store
le rabais	reduction in price
le rayon	shelf, department (of a store)
serré(e)	tight (clothing)
la solde	(clearance) sale
le supermarché	supermarket
la vente	sale

Mots en action

acheter	to buy
amener	to take along
arranger	to arrange
avancer	to advance
balayer	to sweep
la caisse	cash register
charger	to charge, to load
corriger	to correct
effacer	to erase
effrayer	to frighten
élever	to raise, to rear
emmener	to take away
employer	to employ, to use
enlever	to remove, to take off
s'ennuyer	to be bored
envoyer	to send
espérer	to hope
essayer	to try (on)
essuyer	to wipe
forcer	to force
geler	to freeze
jeter	to throw
juger	to judge
lancer	to throw
lever	to raise, to lift
le marchand	merchant
mener	to lead
nettoyer	to clean
partager	to share
payer	to pay (for)
peser	to weigh
peut-être	perhaps, maybe
placer	to place, to put
le pointure	size (shoes, gloves)
pouvoir	to be able to, can
précéder	to precede
se promener	to go for a walk
rejeter	to reject
remplacer	to replace
répéter	to repeat
sécher	to dry
la taille	size
le truc	whatcha-ma-callit

Chapitre Quinze

Structures

Interrogative subject pronouns (**qui, qui est-ce qui, qu'est-ce qui**)

Interrogative direct object pronouns (**qui, qui est-ce que; que, qu'est-ce que**)

Demonstrative adjectives

Connaître (to know; to be acquainted with, to be familiar with)

Objectives

To form and ask appropriate questions using interrogative subject and direct object pronouns

To use demonstrative adjectives

To conjugate and use the irregular verb **connaître**

Rationale

Situation

A la banque introduces students to French currency and the French monetary system, as well as to vocabulary necessary for carrying out a typical tourist banking operation, cashing traveler's checks.

Grammaire

The last major information-eliciting elements--interrogative words for subjects and direct objects--are presented. Much student confusion results from the similarity in form of relative pronouns and these interrogative pronouns. Demonstrative adjectives, while functioning similarly in both French and English, differ in that proximity to the speaker (**this, these**) and distance from the speaker (**that, those**) are normally not indicated in French except emphasis, clarity, or contrast. French has two verbs that represent the single English verb "to know." Distinctions in usage must be made clear.

Strategies

Situation

There is generally no charge in a bank to cash traveler's checks that are already in the currency of the country. To change checks in American dollars (or in another currency) there is a modest charge for the transaction, which is deducted from the amount of the check. A passport must be produced for identification.

Students should practice with currency: recognizing it, counting it, and making change.

Grammaire

There is much potential confusion in forms of the interrogative pronouns and their orthographic "doubles," the relative pronouns. Point out that:

The relative pronoun **qui** functions as subject and refers to both personal and nonpersonal antecedents. The interrogative pronoun **qui** functions only as a subject pronoun for people.

Similarly, the relative pronoun **que** functions as direct object and refers to both personal and nonpersonal antecedents. The interrogative pronoun **que** functions only as a direct object for things.

The long form of the interrogative pronouns may be analyzed as follows:

	REFERENT			FUNCTION	
(PERSON)	**qui**	+ est-ce	(SUBJECT)	**qui**	
(THING)	**que**		(DIRECT OBJECT)		**que**

The interrogative formula **est-ce que** has an alternate form **(est-ce qui)** used only when the interrogation is based on the subject of the question.

The long form **qui est-ce que** is rarely used in everyday conversation.

There is no inversion in questions on the subject when either the short or long forms are used. There is inversion, however, on questions on the direct object when the short forms **(qui/que)** are used. Simple inversion with a noun subject cannot be used with **qui** (direct object), due to ambiguity. However, simple inversion with a noun subject may be used with **que.**

Since French demonstrative adjectives do not distinguish between proximity to the speaker or distance from the speaker, the particles **-ci** (for nearness) and **-là** (for distance) may be added to the noun. American students tend to overuse these particles. Reinforce the concept that context most often determines the interpretation of the demonstrative adjectives. **-ci** is generally not used without **-là.** Stress the alternate form of the masculine singular demonstrative adjective before nouns beginning with a vowel or mute **h.**

With **connaître** and other verbs conjugated similarly, the ^ is used only when the **i** is followed by a **t.**

In the passé composé, **connaître** conveys the meaning of "to meet" (=**faire la connaissance de**).

Distinguish clearly between the uses of **connaître** and **savoir** which can
both mean "to know," but with widely varying uses and meanings. Only
connaître can have a personal noun object, and it can never be
followed by an infinitive. In many cases, either verb could be used
depending on the meaning intended:

Je **connais** ce poème. (I have heard it before.)
Je **sais** ce poème. (I have memorized it.)

Testing

Listening comprehension activities including
personal/nonpersonal questions
subject/direct object interrogatives
singular/plural, masculine/feminine demonstrative adjectives
connaître/savoir distinctions

Answering questions provided and asking appropriate questions to elicit
the answers given

Fill-in-the-blanks with the appropriate interrogative pronouns

Fill-in-the-blanks with
correct form and tense of **connaître**
connaître or **savoir**

Personalized questions using grammar forms in the chapter

Additional Materials

Bank forms

Counter check for practice in writing checks

Up-to-date rate of exchange table

Samples of French (Belgian, Swiss, Canadian, etc.) currency (real or
play money)

Vocabulary:

l'argent (m) de poche	pocket money
l'assurance (f)	insurance
le banquier	banker
la caisse d'épargne	savings bank
le carnet de chèques	checkbook
la carte de crédit	credit card
le chéquier	checkbook
le compte courant	checking account
le compte en banque	bank account
la contrevaleur	equivalent sum
la dépense	expense
les dépenses (fpl)	expenditure

déposer	to deposit
élevé(e)	high (prices)
la facture	bill
les frais (mpl)	expenditure; cost
les frais d'encaissement	charge for cashing a check
mettre	to deposit
le montant	sum
le paiement	payment
remplir	to fill out (a form)
retirer	to withdraw
le revenu	income
la solde	balance
la somme (totale)	amount
le total	amount

Mots en action

le billet	bill (currency)
le bureau de change	money changing office
le caissier	cashier, clerk
le chèque	check
le chèque de voyage	traveler's check
connaître	to know, to be acquainted with
le cours	rate of exchange
le crime	crime
le criminel	criminal
la monnaie	change
la petite monnaie	small change; coins
la pièce (de monnaie)	coin
le récipissé	receipt; stub
reconnaître	to recognize
le stage	internship
toucher	to cash (a check)
voler	to steal
le voleur	thief

Chapitre Seize

Structures

The comparison of adjectives and adverbs

The superlative of adjectives and adverbs

Irregular comparative and superlative forms

The present subjunctive (formation)

Subjunctive: expressions of emotion

Subjunctive: expressions of will or volition

Mettre (to put, to place) (other similar verbs)

Objectives

To form and use both regular and irregular comparative forms of adjectives and adverbs

To form and use both regular and irregular superlative forms of adjectives and adverbs

To form the present subjunctive of regular and irregular verbs

To understand the basic conditions in which the present subjunctive is used

To use the present subjunctive appropriately after verbs and expressions of emotion

To use the present subjunctive appropriately after verbs and expressions of will or volition

To conjugate and use the irregular verb **mettre** and other verbs conjugated similarly

Rationale

Situation

Comment écrit-on une lettre? acquaints students with the various formulae used in writing personal letters and addressing envelopes as well as correct mailing procedures. Most students will likely write personal letters or relatively informal "business" letters requesting information, making reservations, etc., which will roughly follow the same format. Stamps are an excellent source of study for history, culture, etc.

Grammaire

Comparison of both regular and irregular adjectives and adverbs is a very common feature of speech, which is based in a large part on the understanding of adjective forms and adverb derivation and on the placement of such elements in a sentence. The present subjunctive presents many difficulties for language learners due to the infrequent use of this mood in English except in relatively fixed expressions. Students should be made aware of the implications of meaning of the subjunctive mood and the various constraints on its usage. In most instances the subjunctive may be avoided with use of alternate constructions with nonsubjunctive forms. The irregular verb **mettre** and other verbs that follow the same pattern are very common.

Strategies

Situation

Point out the different formulae used in opening and closing letters based on the degee of acquaintance or familiarity between the **expéditeur** and the **destinataire**.

Point out the layout of an envelope mailed to France: the family name is generally written in all capital letters; a comma separates the street number from the name of the street; the "zip code" precedes the city name; the name of the country appears on the line after the city name; **par avion** stickers or the words **par avion** must appear on the envelope for air mail.

In an informal, personal letter, the inside address and date are written as

Chicago, le 9 mai 1984.

Students should write personal letters and address an envelope as an exercise.

Grammaire

Stress that there are three types of comparison:
    superiority: **plus** + adjective or adverb
    equality: **aussi (si)** + adjective or adverb
    inferiority: **moins** + adjective or adverb

Que = "than, as" in comparative degrees. **Que** may be followed by a noun or an emphatic pronoun.

Drill continuously on the use of and distinctions between **bon/bien** and **mauvais/mal** in positive, comparative, and superlative degrees.

Certain adjectives are inherently superlative and have no degrees of comparison: **parfait, unique, supérieur,** etc.

French presents a consistent formation of degrees of comparison (except with highly irregular adjectives and adverbs) while English has a double form: ___, ___-er, ___-est; or ___, more___, most___.

It is advisable to teach the formation of the present subjunctive based on two separate forms of the present indicative:

the **nous** form of the present indicative --> **nous, vous** present subjunctive stems

the **ils** form of the present indicative --> je, **tu, il, ils** present subjunctive stems

While with many verbs these forms are identical, many irregular verbs use two stems: **prendre, boire, recevoir, venir,** etc. **-Er** verb

-75-

spelling changes also occur in the present subjunctive when the tense/person ending is silent.

Categories of verbs and expressions that call for the subjunctive can be set up, but several expressions do not fit well. A mnemonic that might be of some help (only after the subjunctive has been studied) is WEDDINGS. Verbs and expressions that call for the subjunctive include those of:

   Will
   Emotion
   Doubt
   Desire
   Interrogatives
   Negatives
   General characteristics
   Superlatives

Stress the idea that the subjunctive must be used if (1) the verb in the main clause calls for the subjunctive and (2) the subjects of the two verbs in both clauses are different. See Appendices for a list of those verbs requiring **à, de,** or no preposition when followed by a dependent infinitive.

Emphasize that the subjunctive essentially communicates a subjective reaction to factual information.

Sample lists provided in the text are not exhaustive but represent high-frequency expressions that can call for the subjunctive.

Of all verbs and expressions presented in this lesson, stress the use of the subjunctive with **vouloir que** and **avoir peur que,** since these are two of the most common situations in which the subjunctive is used in French.

Note that the constructions used with **permettre, défendre, ordonner** and **empêcher** avoid the subjunctive by using an infinitive construction, even when the subjects of the two verbs are different.

In all situations in this text, the subjunctive occurs in subordinate clauses introduced by **que** (or by conjunctions containing **que).** Warn students that this does not mean that every time **que** is seen that a subjunctive will occur.

Stress the distinction in pronunciation between **il met/ils mettent** and the past participle **mis,** in which feminine past participle agreement will be heard.

Testing

Listening comprehension activities including
   comparative/superlative degrees
   bon/bien; meilleur/mieux discrimination
   present indicative/present subjunctive
   tenses/persons of **mettre**

-76-

Personalized questions and activities using comparative and superlative degrees; sentence completions with present indicative, present subjunctive, or infinitive forms

Fill-in-the-blanks with correct forms of the present subjunctive of the infinitives given

Combining two sentences using either the present subjunctive or infinitive constructions:
   Paul viendra. Je le veux. --> Je veux que Paul vienne.

Fill-in-the-blanks with the appropriate tense/form of **mettre** or verbs in the same family

Using illustrations, writing sentences using positive, comparative, and superlative degrees

Additional Materials

Collections of stamps from francophone countries (Stamps can be put on an outline map of the world for study of francophone areas.)

Sample letters and envelopes written in French

Pen pal situations for students

Sample business letters to illustrate formulae

Various forms from the P.T.T.

Quénelle et Tournaire. La France dans votre poche, "Le savoir écrire"

Vocabulary

aux soins de	in care of
la boîte	box
la boîte en carton	cardboard box
la boîte à lettres	mailbox
le colis	package
la conclusion	conclusion
le courrier	mail
l'étiquette (f)	label
le facteur	mailman
la fermeture	closing
livrer	to deliver
mettre à la poste	to post; to mail
l'ouverture (f)	opening
le poids	weight
(la) poste restante	general delivery
la salutation	salutation
le timbre(-poste)	stamp

Mots en action

admettre to admit
aimer mieux to prefer
l'amitié (f) friendship
aussi...que as...as
collectionner to collect
commetre to commit
le, la destinataire addressee
(s')embrasser to hug, to embrace (each other)
l'enveloppe (f) envelope
s'étonner to be surprised
étrange strange
l'expéditeur (m), **l'expéditrice** (f)   sender
meilleur(e) better
mettre to put, to place
mieux better
ne...pas encore not yet
omettre to omit
ordonner to order
par avion air mail
permettre to permit
pire worse
pis worst
promettre to promise
le sentiment feeling
soumettre to submit
tous les deux both (of them)

Chapitre Dix-Sept

Structures

The subjunctive: doubt and uncertainty

The subjunctive: necessity, importance, and desirability

Ordinal numbers

Fractions

Dates, order of rulers

Croire (to think; to believe)

Objectives

To use the present subjunctive appropriately after verbs and expressions
of doubt and uncertainty

To use the present subjunctive appropriately after impersonal
expressions of necessity, importance, desirability

To form and use ordinal numbers

To form and use fractions

To use cardinal and ordinal numbers appropriately in dates and numerical
order of rulers

To conjugate and use the irregular verb **croire**

Rationale

Situation

Fêtes et traditions introduces students to selected French holidays.
While such cultural information sheds light on the French, American
students are most often called on to explain their own manner of
celebrating. Cross-cultural comparisons and contrasts point out the
danger of drawing cultural stereotypes and increase the student's
awareness of his or her own way of life. Since France is a
predominantly Catholic country, most religious holidays are based on
the church calendar. Also discussed are nonwork days: holidays and
weekends.

Grammaire

Two other uses of the subjunctive are presented--with expressions of
doubt and uncertainty and with impersonal expresions of necessity,
importance, desirability. While illustrating general categories of
use, several nuances and subtleties are introduced that substantiate
the use of the subjunctive to express personal reaction to factual
information. Continuing with numbers, students should be made aware of
the spoken forms of ordinal numbers and fractions and several uses of
these numbers. The irregular verb **croire** (a close synonym of **penser**) is
presented.

Strategies

Situation

Point out the difference between civil and religious holidays.

Try to establish a list of holidays that France and the US celebrate
in common, using a calendar. Point out holidays particular to each
country. Can the existence of these holidays be readily explained?

Have students explain how they celebrate certain holidays, in order to
point out that some cultural traditions are individual in nature and
not national.

Discuss the **Fête nationale française,** July 14. Both the US and France celebrate their national holidays in July. Which celebration is actually older? Why?

Have students find their saint's day.

What is the difference between the American weekend and the French **fin de semaine?** What is considered the weekend in Canada?

Grammaire

Note that expressions of certainty require the indicative while the negative or interrogative forms indicate doubt or uncertainty and therefore require the subjunctive. **Probable,** which is more affirmative in nature than **possible,** requires the indicative, while the latter requires the subjunctive.

The verbs **croire, penser,** and **espérer** require the indicative in affirmative sentences, but may call for the subjunctive or the indicative when negative or interrogative. The use of the subjunctive indicates uncertainty or doubt on the part of the speaker; the indicative indicates the speaker's own opinion with no doubt or uncertainty. This rather subtle nuance is better left for subsequent study. When in doubt, use the subjunctive in these situations.

Stress the obligatory use of the subjunctive after **il faut,** since this is a common occurrence of the subjunctive in everyday usage.

Again, the lists provided are not exhaustive but represent expressions of high-frequency use.

With impersonal expressions, it is important to point out that the impersonal **il** is not the same as the personal pronoun **il.**

Most impersonal expressions are followed by **de** + a dependent infinitive when used in making generalized statements (except for **il faut** and **il vaut mieux,** which are followed directly by infinitives). Frequently, an indirect object pronoun is used with **il faut** + infinitive to avoid the subjunctive construction: **Il me faut partir.**

The formation of ordinal numbers is very regular (except for "first"): **-ième** is added to the base number (note that the final **-e** is omitted in 11-16, 30, 40, 50, 60; that in **neuf,** the final **-f** --> **v;** and that **u** is added to **cinq** in **cinquième.**)

Note that arabic numerals are used with a superscript e (=**-ième**).

Roman numerals are generally used with titles of rulers and the names of centuries: **le XIXe siècle, Louis XIV.**

Point out the relationships between number families: **quart, quatre, quatorze, quarante,** etc.

La moitié = $\frac{1}{2}$ of a whole quantity; **un demi** is a numerical fraction.

Point out agreement rules with **demi**.

Stress that no preposition is used in French to express "on" and "of,"
as in "on the sixteenth of December": **le seize décembre.**

Croire is close in meaning to **penser** except when "to believe" means
"to have faith in."

Testing

Listening comprehension activities including
    subjunctive/indicative with certain expressions and verbs
    subjunctive/infinitive constructions with certain expressions and
       verbs
    recognition of ordinal numbers and fractions (writing down or
       indicating the numbers heard)
    tense/person of **croire**

Adding given impersonal expressions to sentences and making all
necessary changes

Combining two sentences using the present indicative, present
subjunctive, or infinitive constructions

Answering personalized questions calling for the subjunctive,
indicative, or infinitive constructions

Fill-in-the-blanks with the appropriate tense/form of **croire**

Personalized sentence completions with the subjunctive, indicative, or
infinitive constructions

Additional Materials

Various French calendars and **agendas**

Photographs and illustrations of holiday celebrations and traditions

Various French-language greeting cards

Decorations used for holidays

Vocabulary

l'agenda (m)	date book; pocket calendar
le balai	broom
Bon anniversaire.	Happy birthday.
la bûche de Noël	yule log
le chant de Noël	Christmas carol
la citrouille	pumpkin
le fantôme	ghost
la fin de semaine	weekend
Joyeux Noël	Merry Christmas

le sapin   fir tree
la sorcière   witch
la veille   eve

Mots en action

assister à to attend
le bal dance
célébrer to celebrate
le centilitre centiliter
le centimètre centimeter
croire to believe, to think
le décilitre deciliter
le demi half
douter to doubt
douteux(-euse) doubtful
durer to last
la fête holiday, celebration,
    festival
le gramme gram
il importe it is important
il se peut it is possible
il vaut mieux it is better
incertain(e) uncertain

le Jour de l'An New Year's Day
juste just, fair
le kilomètre kilometer
le litre liter
le mètre meter
le milligramme milligram
le millilitre milliliter
Noël/ (m) Christmas
Pâques (m) Easter
se passer to happen
le Père Noël Santa Claus
le quart quarter, fourth
religieux(-euse) religious
sûr(e) sure, certain
le tiers third
la Saint-Valentin Valentine's
Day

Chapitre Dix-huit

Structures

The conditional (formation)

Uses of the conditional (si clauses; for politeness)

Negative expressions

The position of negative expressions (simple and compound tenses;
before an infinitive

Conduire (to drive) (other similar verbs)

Objectives

To form and use the conditional tense

To position and use common negative expressions appropriately

To conjugate and use conduire and similar verbs

Rationale

Situation

The extract from **Astérix chez les Bretons** introduces students to a classic **bande dessinée.** Not only does **Astérix** present a superb example of French humor with its puns, plays on words, satire, and mockery, it also presents a great deal of Gallic history in humorous form.

Grammaire

The conditional is actually two different verb forms: a tense (future-in-the-past) and a mood (used in hypothetical, contrary-to-fact constructions). It is used for softening statements or questions and adding a degree of politeness. French negation differs from that of English on two points: (1) it is comprised of two particles and (2) its one form in French is equivalent to two manners of expression of the same negative idea in English. Rules for use and position vary according to the negative idea expressed. The irregular verb **conduire** and similar verbs are presented.

Strategies

Situation

Point out the **jeux de mots** with both place and personal names.

How can "English" speakers be recognized through their manner of expression?

Give a brief historical overview of Gaul in the time of Julius Caesar.

Point out the Druids, Brittany (and its resemblance to Stonehenge).

Investigate other French **B.D.**s (<u>Lucky Luke</u>), Sempé's cartoons, etc.

Grammaire

The conditional tense is actually the "future-in-the-past," with a use quite similar to that of English. There are <u>no</u> exceptions in the formation of the conditional: future stem + imperfect endings--hence, "future-in-the-past."

As in all situations, do not let students rely on English translations as clues for form or use. "Would," for example, can mean (1) the past tense of "will" (conditional), (2) "used to" (imperfect), (3) to be willing **(vouloir),** (4) present subjunctive: **J'étais surpris qu'il dise cela.**

Emphasize that in hypothetical, contrary-to-fact stataements, if the verb in the **si** clause is in the imperfect, the result clause <u>must</u> be in the conditional, regardless of the form in English. Nonetheless, the use of this construction in French and English is closely parallel.

The conditional tense is used for adding a degree of politeness to statements and questions (as seen in **Chapitre Cinq**).

Negation in French is comprised of two particles: **ne** + a specific negation to convey meaning. **Ne** must appear before the verb (when a verb is present).

Point out the two ways of expressing negation in English: I don't see anything. I see nothing. = **Je ne vois rien.**

Double negatives do not exist in French: **ne** may be used with one or several second negative particles. The double negative problem exists only in English translation.

Drill the use of **ne** + **jamais**.

Emphasize that **Ne...que** is included in the discussion because of the use of **ne**. However, **ne...que** does not call for a reduced partitive article **de**, and **que** has no fixed position except after the verb. **Ne...que** limits or restricts consideration to the noun or phrase following **que**. Translation equivalents are quite varied: "only/nothing but/not anything except", etc. **Ne...que** is a rough synonym of **seulement**. If the predicate of the sentence itself is to be limited, one must use the construction **ne faire que** + an infinitive: **Elle ne fait que manger.**

All negative expressions have affirmative counterparts. This is an important concept for both testing and teaching.

Point out variations in the positioning of negative particles.

Ne is not used when there is no verb, i.e., in one-word answers to questions.

Point out that past participle agreement with **conduire** and similar verbs is heard with feminine preceding direct objects.

Testing

Listening comprehension activities including
  conditional/future
  conditional/imperfect
  affirmative/negative
  forms of **conduire** and similar verbs

Rewriting sentences negatively giving negative counterparts of adverbs and pronouns

Rewriting sentences negatively by inserting the negative expressions given

Completing personalized sentences with **si** clauses or result clauses given

Personalized questions involving negative answers

Fill-in-the-blanks with appropriate conditional forms of the infinitives given

Fill-in-the-blanks with appropriate tense/person of **conduire** and related verbs

Rewriting sentences adding a certain degree of politeness with the conditional tense

Additional Materials

French cartoons and **bandes dessinées**

Other copies of **Astérix**

Vocabulary

après Jésus-Christ	A.D.
avant Jésus-Christ	B.C.
barbare	barbarian
chrétien(ne)	Christian
conquérir	to conquer
le dessin (animée)	cartoon
dessiner	to draw
l'empereur (m)	emperor
(l'impératrice (f))	empress
l'empire (f) romaine	Roman empire
l'envahisseur (m)	invader
l'étandard (m)	standard
la Gaule	Gaul
l'humour (m)	humor
l'invasion (f)	invasion
Jules César	Julius Caesar
païen(ne)	pagan
le Romain	Roman
romain(e)	Roman
Rome	Rome
le vainqueur	victor/winner

Mots en action

l'acte (m) act
l'auteur (m) author
le bande dessinée (la B.D.) comic strip
célèbre famous
le chapitre chapter
conduire to drive
construire to construct, to build
le conte short story
détruire to destroy
le discours speech

l'écrivain (m) writer
l'essai (m) essay
l'histoire (f) story
(ne) jamais never
(ne) ni...ni... neither...nor...
(ne) personne nobody, no one
(ne) plus no more, no longer
(ne) que only
(ne) rien nothing, not anything
l'œuvre (f) work

le **paragraphe** paragraph	le **roman** novel
le **personnage** character	le **romancier** novelist
la **pièce (de théâtre)** play	la **scène** stage, scene
le **poème** poem	le **thème** theme
la **poésie** poetry	**traduire** to translate
le **poète** poet	la **vie** life
produire to produce	

Chapitre Dix-neuf

Structures

Uses of the subjunctive: unique characteristics

Uses of the subjunctive: conjunctions and prepositions

The past subjunctive (formation and uses)

The demonstrative pronoun **ce** (+ modified noun, pronoun, proper name, superlative; + adjective or adverb; + **à** + infinitive)

Recevoir (to receive)

Objectives

To use the subjunctive appropriately in sentences that question the existence of or stress the singular nature of persons or things

To use the subjunctive or infinitive appropriately after certain conjunctions and prepositions

To form and use the past subjunctive appropriately

To distinguish between use of the neuter demonstrative pronoun **ce,** impersonal **il,** and personal pronouns **il(s)/elle(s)**

To conjugate and use the irregular verb **recevoir** and similar verbs

Rationale

Situation

Un voyage en Suisse introduces students to driving in Europe: rules of the road, highways, road signs, and hitchhiking. While there are many similarities, the differences in driving are significant enough to merit a closer investigation, since many travelers will be driving in France.

Grammaire

The use of the subjunctive in situations involving unknown
characteristics, questioned existence, and expression of the singular
nature of persons or things is examined. The occurrence of the
subjunctive after certain conjunctions is the last major category of
the use of this mood. Rules for general use of the subjunctive are still
in effect although the subjunctive may be avoided in certain situations.
The past subjunctive is the only other "working" tense of the
subjunctive in everyday use. The past subjunctive completes the logical
sequencing of tenses in which the subjunctive is used. The neuter
demonstrative pronoun **ce** follows very explicit rules for use in
sentences with relatively similar surface structures: subject pronoun +
être + ... Clear, logical presentation of the use of **ce** can allay many
problems of comprehension. **Recevoir** and other verbs that follow its
conjugation pattern are presented.

Strategies

Situation

Using French road maps to study the highway system, rules of the road,
traffic signs, etc., also affords an opportunity to examine the geography and various regions of France. The **Guide Michelin** (green) is a
good source of information.

A discussion of hitchhiking, backpacking, or bicycling through France
can provide the occasion to discuss youth hostels and inexpensive
student travel in France.

Examine maps of Québec for a similar study of our francophone neigh-
bors.

Grammaire

Note that the subjunctive is often used after **chercher** since this verb
signals a search for something that has not yet been found. **Trouver,**
on the other hand, generally indicates success in the search.

Il n'y a rien/personne both indicate nonexistence and most often call
for the subjunctive.

Conjunctions that call for the subjunctive require a slightly
different view of the rules of subjunctive usage:

> There is generally no verb or expression in the main clause that
> calls for the subjunctive.

> In situations where the subjects of the verbs in the two clauses
> are the same, a preposition + infinitive equivalent to the conjunc-
> tion + subjunctive clause may be used. However, certain conjunc-
> tions have no prepositional counterparts and the subjunctive must
> be used.

Stress particularly the correct use of **avant que** and **pour que,** which are among the most common expressions calling for use of the subjunctive.

Point out the use of the expletive (pleonastic) **ne** in certain subjunctive expressions for passive recognition only.

The formation of the past subjunctive is based on mastery-level knowledge of the **passé composé: être/avoir** as auxiliaries, past participle formation and agreement, placement of negatives and object pronouns, etc., plus the present subjunctive of **être** and **avoir.**

Use of the past subjunctive is clearly limited and is based solely on the time relationship between the verbs in the independent and subordinate clauses. This clear sequence of tenses, coupled with context, allows for accurate interpretation of meaning.

Rules for correct use of **ce,** impersonal **il,** or the personal pronouns **il(s)/elle(s)** can be clearly presented as follows:

(a)   If what follows **être** could function as the subject of a sentence (if it is a noun or pronoun), **ce** is used as the subject.

(b)   If what follows **être** cannot function as the subject of a sentence (if it is an adjective, adverb, or prepositional phrase), then the appropriate personal pronoun subject **(il(s)/elle(s))** must be used.

Unmodified nouns of nationality, profession, religion, political affiliation, etc., function technically as adjectives, so the rule presented in (b) above is still valid. However, when such nouns are modified, even by a definite or indefinite article, they function as nouns and rule (a) above is in effect.

In situations in which **ce** or impersonal **il** may function as the subject of **être, ce** refers to a preceding idea, phrase, or clause that has no gender; il refers forward in the sentence to the true subject which follows (generally an infinitive phrase introduced by **de** or a relative clause introduced by **que).** In the case where **ce** or **il** is followed by an infinitive, **ce** calls for the use of **à** + infinitive while **il** calls for the use of **de.**

Remind students that nouns of nationality are capitalized; adjectives of nationality are not.

In verbs ending in **-cevoir,** a cedilla must be placed under the **c** whenever it is followed by **a, o, u** to retain the soft (s) sound of the **c.**

Point out the distinction between **apercevoir** and **s'apercevoir de** and mention **remarquer:**

    apercevoir   to notice by sight, to catch a glimpse of (It may not be followed by a clause introduced by **que.)**

s'apercevoir de	to notice mentally, to become aware of, to realize (It may only refer to facts; concrete things cannot be the subject of **s'apercevoir de.**)
remarquer	to notice (to note, to observe, to pay attention to) (**Remarquer** may be followed by concrete or abstract nouns and may be used in the imperative.)

Testing

Listening comprehension activities including
  present/past subjunctive
  past subjunctive/passé composé
  subjunctive/indicative in sentences
  ce/il as subject of the sentence
  distinction of forms/tenses of **recevoir** and related verbs

Combining sentences by connecting them with conjunctions (+ subjunctive) or prepositions (+ infinitive)

Selection of present/past subjunctive to complete sentences logically

Fill-in-the-blanks with **ce,** impersonal **il,** or **il(s)/elle(s)** as needed

Completion of personalized sentences using conjunctions (+ subjunctive) or prepositions (+ infinitive)

Fill-in-the-blanks with appropriate tense/person of **recevoir** and related verbs

Additional Materials

Road maps of France and Canada (Esso, Total, ELF)

Guide Michelin (green and red)

Charts of international road signs

International driver's license

"Mille bornes" (card game)

Quénelle et Tournaire. La France dans votre poche, sections on highway travel, cars, etc.

"Routes de France" (card game), Gessler Publishing company (No. 4725)

"Memory—Code de la route" (game with international road signs), Gessler Publishing Company (No. 8737)

Travel guides for students

Vocabulary

la batterie	battery
le capot	hood
changer de vitesses	to change gears
le chauffeur	driver
le clignotant	signal light
le coffre	trunk
la crevaison	flat tire
démarrer	to start (a car)
l'essuie-glace (m)	windshield wiper
le frein	brake
le gazoil	diesel fuel
l'huile (f)	oil
le klaxon	horn
le moteur	engine
le pare-brise	windshield
le parking	parking lot
parquer	to park
la plaque d'immatriculation	license plate, tag
le pneu	tire
la pompe (à essence)	gas pump
le poste d'essence	gas station
le radiateur	radiator
le réservoir	(gas) tank
le rétroviseur	rearview mirror
la roue	wheel
le siège	seat (of a car)
stationner	to park
le tuyau	hose

Mots en action

afin que so that, in order to
à moins que unless
apercevoir to see suddenly; to see
   at a distance; to discover
s'apercevoir de to notice
l'autoroute (f) superhighway, turnpike
l'auto-stoppeur (M),
   l'auto-stoppeuse (f) hitchhiker
avant que before
bien que although
décevoir to deceive
de crainte que for fear that
jusqu'à ce que until
marcher to run, to work (machines)
où que wherever, no matter where

pour que so that, in order to
pourvu que provided that
prudent(e) careful
qui que whoever, no matter who(m)
quoi que whatever, no
   matter what
quoique although
recevoir to receive
la route road
sans que without
seul(e) alone
la station-service service station
la vitesse autorisée speed limit
le volant steering wheel

Chapitre Vingt

Structures

The interrogative adjective **quel**

Relative pronouns: preposition + **qui**

The relative pronoun **lequel**

Devoir (to owe; must)

Uses of **devoir**

Objectives

To use the interrogative adjective **quel** in both interrogations and exclamations

To use the relative pronoun **qui** as a personal object of a preposition

To use a form of the relative pronoun **lequel** as a nonpersonal object of a preposition

To conjugate **devoir**

To use forms of **devoir** appropriately in sentences indicating obligation or necessity

Rationale

Situation

Le mariage introduces students to marriage customs in France and to the basic concept of the family.

Grammaire

The use of relative pronouns as objects of prepositions is the last major category of relative pronoun use. Subsequent discussions of relative pronouns present alternate forms and shortcuts in usage. The interrogative adjective **quel** follows normal adjective agreement rules. It may be used both in interrogatives and in exclamations. The irregular verb **devoir** is highly complex in its use since meaning changes in the various tenses.

Strategies

Situation

Using **Le mariage** as a point of departure, class discussions can center on the comparisons and contrasts concerning the concept of the family in both France and the United States: roles, working parents, family size, etc.

Discussion of marriage can also cover religious and civil ceremonies and the role of religion in the French family.

Grammaire

The interrogative adjective **quel** presents very few problems in its use. Emphasize that **quel** may either be followed directly by the noun it modifies or separated from the noun by **être**. In either case, **quel** must agree with the noun it modifies.

As an exclamation, in the singular <u>quel</u> means "what a(n)..."--the indefinite article is not needed.

Quel may be preceded by a preposition, but there is no contracted form.

Note that whether the antecedent is personal or nonpersonal must be taken into account when dealing with relative pronoun selection as objects of prepositions; **qui** may only be used for people and **lequel** basically for things.

Stress the fact that forms of **lequel** contract with the prepositions **à** and **de**.

Indirect objects (as objects of **à**) and the pronoun **y** are included in the discussion of relative pronouns as objects of a preposition.

Mastery of the use of relative pronouns studied thus far is sufficient for effective communication. Any subsequent study of relative pronouns will offer alternate (although more commonly used) forms.

Stress the distinction between the two expressions of necessity or obligation, **devoir** and **il faut**:

Devoir signals an obligation from within, a moral or personal obligation.

Il faut signals an obligation imposed from outside or duty to someone else.

When followed by a noun, **devoir** means "to owe"; followed by an infinitive, it conveys the idea of duty or obligation. Note that in this latter meaning, tense shift indicates different perspectives on obligation, necessity, or probability.

Testing

Listening comprehension activities including
   personal/nonpersonal relative pronoun antecedents
   the use of **quel** as interrogative or in exclamation
   implications of meaning of **devoir** in various tenses
   recognition of various tenses/forms of **devoir**

Combining pairs of sentences substituting appropriate prepositions and relative pronouns

Fill-in-the-blanks with appropriate forms of **devoir**

Personalized questions involving the use of prepositions and relative pronouns, various forms of **devoir**

Additional Materials

Wedding invitations and newspaper announcements

Vocabulary

le baptême	baptism
la belle-fille	daughter-in-law
la belle-mère	mother-in-law
la bru	daughter-in-law
élever	to rear (children)
enceinte	pregnant
le faire-part	announcement
le foyer	home
le gendre	son-in-law
la jalousie	jealousy
les jumeaux (mpl)	twins
le ménage	household
le prénom	Christian (first) name

Mots en action

l'autorité (f) authority
la cérémonie ceremony
le couple couple
devoir to owe; must
le divorce divorce
l'emploi (m) job

les fiançailles (fpl) engagement
la lune de miel honeymoon
le mariage marriage
le rapport relationship
tomber amoureux(-euse) de to fall in love with

Chapitre Vingt et un

Structures

Interrogative pronouns with prepositions (personal and nonpersonal)

The interrogative pronoun **lequel**

The demonstrative pronoun **celui** (with definite antecedents)

The demonstrative pronouns **ceci** and **cela**

The pluperfect (formation; uses)

Suivre (to follow; to take a course)

Objectives

To form and ask appropriate questions using prepositions + personal and nonpersonal interrogative pronouns

To form and ask appropriate questions using forms of **lequel**

To use demonstrative pronouns with specific antecedents

To use indefinite demonstrative pronouns

To form and use the pluperfect tense

To conjugate and use the irregular verb **suivre**

Rationale

Situation

Les débouchés introduces students to the importance of foreign language ability in careers other than teaching and interpreting. Today's shrinking globe and the rise of international business at all levels illustrate even more clearly the need for foreign language ability coupled with other skills.

Grammaire

The last major categories of interrogatives--interrogative pronouns with prepositions and **lequel**--complete the study of interrogation. All types of information can now be sought. Demonstrative pronouns are necessary features of everyday language use that reduce the repetitive nature of sentences of beginning students through appropriate pronoun substitution. The pluperfect tense provides a necessary degree of shading for the adequate expression of time relationships in the past. The irregular verb **suivre** is commonly used when speaking of taking courses--an appropriate topic.

Strategies

Situation

Have students find classified ads calling for knowledge of French.
What types of jobs are available? What other skills, if any, are
called for in addition to a foreign language? Where are the jobs
located? What degree of knowledge of French is called for?

Investigate, through surveys, interviews, or studies, the need for
foreign language abilities in business careers.

See Additional Materials for informational sources concerning careers.

Grammaire

Point out that any conversational English question that ends with a
preposition must begin with the preposition in French.

Stress the distinction between personal and nonpersonal interrogative
pronouns.

Quoi is simply an alternate form of **que** that occurs in strong positions (after prepositions or alone), similar to me/moi, te/toi.

Students must rely on the verb used in French to determine the
appropriate preposition.

Lequel as an interrogative pronoun replaces questions using **quel** + a
personal or nonpersonal noun. **Lequel** must be in the same gender and
number as the noun it replaces.

Do not forget that **lequel** will contract with **à** and **de** in questions
beginning with those prepositions.

Remind students that **lequel** means "which" in the sense of "which
one(s)."

Demonstrative pronouns replace demonstrative adjectives + personal or
nonpersonal nouns. Demonstrative pronouns with definite antecedents
may never stand alone. They must be followed by **-ci** or **-là,** a
prepositional phrase, or a relative clause.

Demonstrative pronouns + **-ci/-là** are used to indicate "the former" and
"the latter." Note that in French, the demonstrative pronoun + **-ci**
occurs first and refers to the last item mentioned (the latter). This
can be confusing to students.

Point out the use of celui de Jean = John's.

The word **ça** is a conversational "contraction" of cela.

Ceci refers to something that is to follow, **cela** to something that has
already been mentioned.

The pluperfect tense means "more past than past" (<u>parfait</u>/perfect = past). Its formation illustrates this: the auxiliary verb in the imperfect tense + past participle.

Suivre as an irregular verb is most commonly used in speaking of courses taken. Point out the ambiguity of **je suis** (from both **suivre** and **être**).

Testing

Listening comprehension activities including
    personal/nonpersonal questions using interrogative pronouns with
      prepositions
    gender/number of referents in questions with **lequel**
    gender/number of referents of demonstrative pronouns
    recognition of forms/tenses of **suivre**

The appropriate creation of questions based on answers given

Fill-in-the-blanks with appropriate forms of the pluperfect

Personalized activities including use of the pluperfect, demonstrative pronouns, and **suivre**

Additional Materials

Classified ads for jobs

Patricia L. Gallo and Frank Sedwick. <u>French for Careers: Conversational Perspectives</u>. Boston: Heinle & Heinle Publishers

Theodore Huebener. <u>Opportunities in Foreign Language Careers</u>. Louisville, KY: Vocational Guidance Manuals, 1976

Edward Bourgoin. <u>Foreign Languages and Your Career.</u> ACTFL Materials Center

<u>The ACTFL Foreign Language Career Education Packet</u>. ACTFL Materials Center

Vocabulary:

les affaires (fpl)	business
la direction	management
l'entreprise (f)	venture; firm
les gages (mpl)	wages
gagner	to earn
les petites annonces (f)	classified ads
S.A. (Société anonyme)	corporation
le salaire	salary
la technologie	technology

Mots en action

l'avocat (m), l'avocate (f) lawyer
la carrière career
le coiffeur, la coiffeuse hair stylist
le conseil (piece of) advice
le conseiller adviser
le débouché opportunity
la diplomatie diplomacy
le directeur, la directrice director
le droit law
l'électricien (m) electrician
l'enseignement (m) teaching
la facilité gift, talent
la formation training

l'infirmier (m), l'infirmière (f)
   nurse
l'ingénieur (m) engineer
l'interprète (m,f) interpreter
le journalisme journalism
le juge judge
le menuisier carpenter
l'orientation (f) direction,
   guidance
le pompier firefighter
le poste job, position
réfléchir to think
le, la secrétaire secretary
le technicien, la technicienne
   technician

Chapitre Vingt-deux

Structures

The past conditional (formation)

Uses of the past conditional (as in English; with **si** clauses)

Si clauses: summary

Causative **faire**

The present participle (formation; as adjective ; as verbal)

Boire (to drink)

Objectives

To form and use appropriately the past conditional

To use the appropriate sequence of tenses in conditional sentences

To use the causative **faire** construction

To form and use the present participle

To conjugate and use the irregular verb **boire**

Rationale

Situation

Comment refuser is based on functional/notional principles, in that a theme is set and appropriate structures are introduced to be used in such a situation. Styles and levels of language are examined. Foreigners find it difficult to react in situations calling for use of the target language due to insufficient training in the affective use of grammar.

Grammaire

The past conditional is used primarily in hypothetical, contrary-to-fact sentences containing **si** clauses in the pluperfect tense. A chart summarizes the complete sequence of tenses in **si** clause sentences. The causative **faire** construction, while relatively common, is rather intricate in its use. The present participle is a verbal--as are infinitives and past participles--a form derived from a verb but which has other grammatical functions in a sentence. Students should be acquainted with its form and uses. The irregular verb **boire** is presented.

Strategies

Situation

By creating a situation similar to that illustrated, have students react in English to individuals of all sorts, in order to illustrate appropriate language use and register (a phenomenon that students take for granted in their own language). Point out the similarity of reactions.

Illustrate the **Situation** with appropriate gestures.

Point out the fact that Americans in general walk around in a "personal bubble of space." When someone encroaches into another's space, Americans withdraw and say "excuse me": accidentally bumping into someone on the street, entering a door at the same time, going to one's seat at the movies or theater, etc. Most Europeans get close to those they are speaking with and frequently touch them. Examine other such phenomena.

Grammaire

Point out that the past conditional must be used in the result clause when the **si** clause contains a pluperfect tense, regardless of what is said in English.

Such **si**-clause sentences (with the pluperfect/past conditional) are contrary to fact because, since the condition set forth in the **si** clause was not met, the result clause did not take place.

Point out the chart that summarizes the sequence of tenses in the three types of **si**-clause sentences:

present/future
imperfect/conditional
pluperfect/past conditional

The sequence of tenses actually closely parallels that of English. Note that a future form or any form based on the future can never occur in the **si** clause.

The causative **faire** + infinitive construction may be split only by negatives, inverted subject pronouns, and object pronouns in affirmative imperative constructions. In other secondary auxiliary + infinitive constructions, this is not the case since object pronouns, for instance, can be placed before the verb of which they are the objects.

Due to the nature of the causative **faire** construction, direct objects of **faire** must become indirect objects in form while objects of the infinitive remain direct object in form.

Verbs of perception (**voir, entendre, regarder, écouter, sentir**) and **laisser** + infinitive may follow the same rules as causative **faire** or may be considered as two separate verbs with respective objects:

I heard the children singing: **Jai entendu chanter les enfants.**
   J'ai entendu les enfants chanter.

Remind students that the past participle of **faire** in the causative construction never shows agreement.

The present participle has a limited sphere of use: as an adjective or as a replacement for a clause. Although it is equivalent to English words ending in **-ing**, the present participle is not used (1) in progressive verb forms (I am going) or (2) in constructions such as "We watched them playing." In (1) the present indicative, imperfect, present subjunctive, or **être en train de** + infinitive is used; in (2) an infinitive is used.

The present participle without **en** is often a replacement for a clause beginning with a relative pronoun: **J'ai rencontré Paul <u>sortant du cinéma</u> = <u>qui sortait du cinéma.</u>**

The irregular verb **boire** indicates the physical act of drinking, just as **manger** indicates the act of eating (chewing and swallowing). **Prendre** or another verb is frequently used:

What do you want to drink?   **Que voulez-vous prendre?**
He is eating lunch.   **Il déjeune.**

Testing

Listening comprehension activities including
  conditional/past conditional
  pluperfect/past conditional
  causative/noncausative constructions
  present participle with and without **en** (to whom do they refer?)
  recognition of forms of **boire**

Completion of personalized sentences with **si** clauses

Rewriting sentences with causative **faire**

Rewriting sentences using causative **faire**, replacing object nouns with pronouns

Fill-in-the-blanks of sentences with **si** clauses, using appropriate tenses and forms of infinitives

Rewriting sentences replacing clauses with present participle forms

Fill-in-the-blanks with appropriate tenses/forms of **boire**

Additional Materials

Catherine Maley. <u>Dans le vent</u>. Holt, Rinehart, Winston. See pages 165-172, "Comment répondre," for an active list of affective statements and reactions.

Vocabulary

l'accord (m)	agreement
l'avis (m)	advice (warning)
la colère	anger, rage
la compassion	compassion
la défense	forbidding
le désaccord	disagreement
le doute	doubt
en avoir ras-le-bol	to be fed up
l'ennui (m)	boredom
l'enthousiasme (m)	enthusiasm
l'incompréhension (f)	lack of understanding
l'intérêt (m)	interest
la joie	joy
le manque (de)	lack (of)
négatif (-ive)	negative
l'opinion (f)	opinion
positif (-ive)	positive
le sarcasme	sarcasm
la surprise	surprise

Mots en action

aimable kind, nice
boire to drink
exprimer to express
incroyable unbelievable
l'invité (m), l'invitée (f) guest
justifier to justify
odieux(-euse) disgusting, unbearable
poli(e) polite

prendre un verre to have a drink
le refus refusal
remercier to thank
rigolo very funny
la soirée dansante dance
sympa (invariable, from sympathique)
  nice
le type guy

Chapitre Vingt-trois

Structures

Possessive pronouns

The passive voice

Active voice versus passive voice

The relative pronoun dont

The relative adverb où

The relative pronouns ce qui, ce que, and ce dont

Craindre (to fear) (other similar verbs)

Objectives

To recognize and use possessive pronouns

To form sentences in both the passive voice and by using active voice equivalents for the passive

To use dont as a relative pronoun replacement for constructions using de + object

To use où as a relative pronoun replacement for expressions of time and location

To use ce qui, ce que, ce dont appropriately as relative pronoun forms with no antecedent

To conjugate and use the irregular verb craindre and similar verbs

Rationale

Situation

Départ de Charles-de-Gaulle introduces students to international air travel and related vocabulary. Leaving France can be a sad but rewarding time since, having successfully completed **Accent**, they can now travel to and in francophone countries with much less fear and trepidation because they can now function in another language.

Grammaire

Possessive pronouns are quite easily replaced by other constructions, so a passive knowledge of their forms is sufficient at this stage. The passive voice is used much more commonly in English than in French. In French, there are several possibilities for avoiding the passive by using active voice equivalents. The relative pronouns presented in this lesson are simply alternate means of expression. **Craindre** and similar verbs are presented.

Strategies

Situation

Explain procedures for leaving a foreign country--customs (allowances, limits, and restrictions), reconversion of currency, location of airports, etc.

If available, use publications of the Aéroport Charles de Gaulle (**Je pars/J'arrive**) for study.

Using customs pamphlets from Canada, France, and the US, discuss what happens at customs, what can be brought back, etc.

Grammaire

Teach passive recognition of possessive pronoun forms by having students rephrase sentences using alternate, more common constructions indicating possession.

Point out the contraction of the definite article in possessive pronoun forms with **à** and **de**.

In the passive voice, the subject "receives" the action of the verb and the agent (introduced by **par** or **de**) "performs the action." Only the direct object of an active sentence can become the subject of a passive sentence. Therefore, the typically English construction "He was given a car by his father" has no direct equivalent in French.

The tense of **être** in a passive construction must be the same as the verb (indicated by the past participle in the passive sentence) in the equivalent active form.

Past participles in true passive constructions function as adjectives and must therefore agree in gender and in number with the subject of the passive sentence.

The active construction with **on** may be used only when (a) the agent is not expressed and (b) when the understood agent is a person.

Reflexive equivalents of the passive voice are most common in expressions such as **Cela ne se fait pas** and **Cela ne se dit pas.**

Dont represents any relative pronoun construction using **de + qui/lequel** when **de** means "of."

The subject of the relative clause must always follow **dont** directly, regardless of the English construction.

Since **dont** includes **de**, it is a replacement for possessive adjectives: **son = de lui, d'elle.**

Point out that **dont** may never be used as an interrogative word.

Où is used to replace any preposition of location (most commonly **à** and **dans**) + object except for the preposition **de**, in which case **d'où** must be used.

Où may be used as a replacement for any specified time as indicated by the use of the definite article: **le jour où.** In all other cases, use **que** (=when): **un jour que.**

Ce qui, ce que, ce dont are used when (a) there is no antecedent for the relative pronoun (**ce** functions as the needed antecedent) or (b) the antecedent is an idea, phrase, or clause.

In most cases, "that (of) which" can be inserted into the English sentence to verify the use of **ce.**

Point out the pronunciation of **-gn-** in forms of **craindre** and similar verbs; it is roughly equivalent to the middle sound in the English words <u>onion</u>, <u>canyon</u>.

Craindre is less commonly used than its synonym **avoir peur de.**

Testing

Listening comprehension activities including
  active/passive constructions
  singular/plural, masculine/feminine possessive pronouns
  relative pronouns with and without antecedents
  time/place with **où**
  recognition of forms of **craindre** and similar verbs

Combining pairs of sentences with appropriate relative pronoun forms

Rewriting sentences using possessive pronoun replacements

Fill-in-the-blanks with the correct relative pronouns

Rewriting passive sentences in the active voice

Fill-in-the-blanks with appropriate tense/forms of **craindre** and similar verbs

Additional Materials

Magazines provided free on airplanes (Air France <u>Atlas</u>)

Customs brochures and pamphlets

Realia from airline companies

Vocabulary

l'aile (f)	wing
l'avion (m) à réaction	jet
boucler	to buckle
la charrette	cart
confirmer	to confirm
débarquer	to deplane, to get off
s'embarquer	to get on board
faire signe (de la main)	to wave
le jet	jet
le mal de l'air	airsickness
les papiers (mpl)	documents
le passager, la passagère	passenger
la passerelle	gangway
la piste	runway
la porte	gate
la poussette	cart
réclamer	to pick up, to claim baggage
le siège	seat
le visa (d'entrée)	visa

Mots en action

l'agence (f) de voyages travel agency
attacher to buckle, to fasten
atterrir to land (plane)
l'atterrissage (m) landing
la carte d'embarquement boarding pass
craindre to fear
déclarer to declare
décoller to take off (plane)
la douane customs
le douanier customs officer

éteindre to extinguish
fouiller to search, to go through
l'hôtesse (f) de l'air flight attendant
joindre to join
peindre to paint
plaindre to pity
se plaindre de to complain about
prendre l'avion to fly (persons)
rejoindre to meet; to join
voler to fly

Chapitre Un

I.

A. 1. la banque
2. le café/le restaurant
3. le cinéma
4. l'école/le lycée
5. le musée
6. le bureau de poste/la poste
7. la gare
8. la plage

B.

II.

A. 1. C'est une avenue.
2. C'est un cinéma.
3. C'est une plage.
4. C'est un hôpital.
5. C'est une place.
6. C'est une piscine.
7. C'est un musée/C'est une bibliothèque.
8. C'est un lycée.
9. C'est une banque.
10. C'est une église.

B. 1. Il y a une voiture.
2. Il y a des jardins.
3. Il y a des professeurs.
4. Il y a une gare.
5. Il y a des amies.
6. Il y a une femme.
7. Il y a des écoles.
8. Il y a un agent de police.
9. Il y a des magasins.
10. Il y a un café.

C. 1. Oui, voilà le plan.
2. Oui, voilà les écoles.
3. Oui, voilà l'hôtel.
4. Oui, voilà la poste.
5. Oui, voilà les résidences.
6. Oui, voilà le lycée.
7. Oui, voilà les théâtres.
8. Oui, voilà l'université.
9. Oui, voilà l'homme.
10. Oui, voilà les restaurants.

D. 1. a   6. a
    2. avons   7. as
    3. ont   8. a
    4. ai   9. ont
    5. avez   10. a

E. 1. Elle a une voiture.   4. Ils ont des amis.
    2. Elle a une gare.   5. Il a un café.
    3. Elles ont des résidences. 6. Il a un magasin.

F. 1. de   6. Aux
    2. au   7. à l'
    3. au   8. du
    4. du   9. de la
    5. du   10. des

G. 1. Il y a un hôtel dans la ville.
    2. Jean-Paul et Louise ont une maison près de l'école.
    3. Suivez la rue jusqu'au magasin et tournez à droite.
    4. Anne a une camarade de chambre.
    5. Il y a deux maisons à côté du parc.
    6. La maison du professeur, s'il vous plaît?
    7. Tout le monde a un ami à l'école.
    8. J'ai un plan de l'université.
    9. Le marché est près du bureau de poste (près de la poste).
   10. Voilà ta voiture--derrière la résidence!

Chapitre Deux

I.
A. 1. le papier   5. la table
    2. le crayon   6. le livre
    3. le stylo (à bille)   7. la note
    4. la chaise   8. la fenêtre

B. 1. le tableau   5. enthousiaste
    2. stupide   6. le disque
    3. le doigt   7. la chaise
    4. au revoir

II.
A. 1. C'est le cahier du garçon.
    2. C'est la chaise de l'étudiant.
    3. C'est le bureau du professeur.
    4. C'est la voiture du monsieur.
    5. C'est le jardin de l'hôtel.
    6. C'est la résidence de l'université.
    7. Ce sont les notes des étudiants.
    8. C'est la maison de la dame.
    9. Ce sont les crayons des jeunes filles.
   10. Ce sont les salles de classe du lycée.

B.

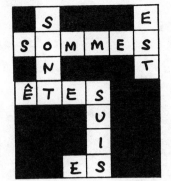

C. 1. Sept et deux font neuf.
    2. Trois et cinq font huit.
    3. Six et un font sept.
    4. Huit et deux font dix.
    5. Quatre et trois font sept.
    6. Cinq et quatre font neuf.
    7. Six et trois font neuf.
    8. Sept et trois font dix.

D. 1. Non, Paul n'est pas ici.
    2. Non, je n'ai pas d'examen.
    3. Non, ça ne va pas.
    4. Non, on n'est pas à la porte.
    5. Non, je n'ai pas de dollar.
    6. Non, ils ne sont pas devant la poste.
    7. Non, deux et trois ne font pas six.
    8. Non, il n'y a pas de piscine à l'université.
    9. Non, je ne suis pas malade.
    10. Non, vous n'avez pas de devoirs aujourd'hui.

E. 1. Le Louvre est à Paris?
       Est-ce que le Louvre est à Paris?
    2. Il y a un tableau dans la salle de classe?
       Est-ce qu'il y a un tableau dans la salle de classe?
    3. Nous avons des devoirs?
       Est-ce que nous avons des devoirs?
    4. Le marché est à côté de la place?
       Est-ce que le marché est à côté de la place?
    5. Tu as un crayon?
       Est-ce que tu as un crayon?
    6. Le monsieur a une femme?
       Est-ce que le monsieur a une femme?
    7. Les étudiants ont des leçons?
       Est-ce que les étudiants ont des leçons?
    8. Le bureau du professeur est devant la classe?
       Est-ce que le bureau du professeur est devant la classe?
    9. Elle a un Coca?
       Est-ce qu'elle a un Coca?
    10. J'ai tort?
       Est-ce que j'ai tort?

F. 1. Il y a un cinéma à côté de l'école.
    2. Bonjour, Georges, Comment allez-vous? --Assez bien, merci.
    3. Avez-vous deux stylos?/As-tu deux stylos?
    4. Au revoir, Jean. A plus tard!
    5. Nous sommes en classe et nous avons un examen aujourd'hui.
    6. Le camarade de chambre de Paul est sympathique.
    7. Il n'y a pas de note sur le devoir de Marie.

8. A qui est ce cahier? --Il est à Henri.
9. Tu n'es pas dans la classe de Caroline? --Si.
10. Il n'y a pas de fenêtres dans la salle de classe. --C'est dommage.

Chapitre Trois

I.

A.
1. rouge
2. gris
3. jaune
4. blanc

5. rose/rouge
6. noir
7. rouge/jaune/vert

B.

II.

A.
1. C'est une porte blanche.
2. J'ai une cassette américaine.
3. Ce sont des jeunes filles méchantes.
4. Elle a une nouvelle amie.
5. Voilà les étudiantes blondes.
6. C'est une longue rue.
7. Il habite un vieil hôtel.
8. La copine est gentille.
9. Quel bel homme!
10. Voici une grande ville russe.

B.
1. Le français est une belle langue.
2. J'ai un autre examen important.
3. Elle porte de nouvelles chaussures.
4. Paris est une grande ville française.
5. J'ai une petite voiture bleue.
6. Elle a de bonnes amies étrangères.
7. Ils ont des vêtements laids.
8. Ils écoutent de vieux disques intéressants.
9. Ce sont de jolis jardins anglais.
10. J'aime les plantes vertes.

C. 1. aimons   5. écoutent   9. regardes   13. téléphone
   2. portes   6. Joue   10. entrent   14. Parle
   3. ouvre   7. dépense   11. offre   15. quittez
   4. Habitez   8. nageons   12. Cherchez   16. voyageons

D. 1. Parlez-vous français?   6. Marche-t-il derrière Michèle?
   2. Aimez-vous la télévision?   7. N'es-tu pas intelligent?
   3. N'a-t-il pas de voiture?   8. Désirent-ils voyager?
   4. Porte-t-elle un t-shirt?   9. Oublie-t-elle l'examen?
   5. Travaillons-nous en classe?   10. Restez-vous à la maison?

F. 1. Nous avons un long examen difficile maintenant.
   2. Emprunte-t-elle un dollar à Jean?
   3. Ils habitent une grande maison blanche.
   4. J'offre un Coca aux étudiants. Aiment-ils les Cocas?
   5. Le professeur a une vieille voiture noire.
   6. Regardez-vous ce bel homme?
   7. Nous mangeons à l'université.
   8. Les nouveaux étudiants arrivent aujourd'hui. Ils cherchent les
      résidences.
   9. Est-ce que les parents de Marie téléphonent au professeur?
  10. Je ne désire pas prêter de stylo à l'étudiant.

Chapitre Quatre

I.
A. 1. le chapeau
   2. la chemise, la blouse, le pull, l'anorak
   3. la ceinture
   4. le pantalon
   5. la chaussure, la chaussette

B. 1. bateau   4. couteau
   2. gâteau   5. oiseau
   3. drapeau   6. panneau

C. 1. paresseux   5. choix
   2. curieux   6. faux
   3. prix   7. roux
   4. heureux   8. studieux/sérieux

II.
A. 1. Leurs cheveux sont roux.   6. Je sors de leur maison.
   2. C'est son fils.   7. Nous voyageons dans votre
   3. Voici ma photo.   voiture.
   4. C'est son enfant.   8. Voilà son amie.
   5. Paul porte son anorak.   9. J'ai leurs cadeaux.
                                     10. Je regarde sa télévision.

B. 1. Ce sont mes livres.
   C'est mon amie.
   C'est mon copain.
   C'est ma plante.

2. C'est ta chaussure.
   C'est ton cahier.
   Ce sont tes notes.
   C'est ton école.

3. C'est sa voiture.
   C'est son crayon.
   Ce sont des disques.
   C'est son église.

4. C'est son gâteau.
   Ce sont ses photos.
   C'est sa fille.
   C'est son ami.

5. C'est notre travail.
   Ce sont nos professeurs.
   C'est notre banque.

6. C'est votre fils.
   Ce sont vos souliers.
   C'est votre chemise.

7. C'est leur classe.
   Ce sont leurs examens.
   C'est leur stylo.

8. Ce sont leurs blouses.
   C'est leur bikini.
   C'est leur devoir.

C. 1. Mes fils sont heureux.
   2. Les couteaux sont dangereux.
   3. Les oiseaux sont nerveux.
   4. Ses neveux sont studieux.
   5. Les jeux sont sérieux.
   6. Les manteaux sont épais.
   7. Les prix sont faux.
   8. Les gâteaux sont délicieux.

D. 1. choisis
   2. obéit
   3. punissent
   4. réussis
   5. remplissons
   6. choisissez
   7. punit
   8. finissent
   9. Finis
   10. obéissent

E. 1. sert
   2. dormons
   3. sortent
   4. Mens
   5. servez
   6. Sort
   7. partent
   8. ment
   9. Dormez
   10. partons

F. 1. onze francs
   2. vingt francs
   3. dix-neuf francs
   4. treize francs
   5. quinze francs
   6. douze francs
   7. seize francs
   8. quatorze francs
   9. dix-huit francs
   10. dix-sept francs

G. 1. Est-ce que votre train part de Paris aujourd'hui?
   2. Nous désirons deux morceaux de gâteau.
   3. Ils finissent leurs repas maintenant.
   4. Ses fils sont très paresseux.
   5. J'aime dormir sur la plage.
   6. Ses cheveux sont roux.
   7. Quelquefois, je sors de la classe avant l'heure.
   8. Est-ce que les petits enfants obéissent à leurs parents?
   9. Est-ce que les étudiants ici sont très sérieux ou sont-ils paresseux?
   10. Jean-Paul porte mes chaussures!

I.

B. 1. beaucoup/trop
    2. moins
    3. une paire
    4. peu

    5. un verre
    6. beaucoup
    7. plus
    8. peu de

II.

C. 1. Voilà de méchants garçons.
    2. Nous voulons des cerises rouges.
    3. Il regarde de vieux films.
    4. Voici de nouveaux étudiants.
    5. Nous étudions de longs livres.

    6. Ils cherchent des hôtels modernes.
    7. Tu commandes du bon café.
    8. Voilà de hautes résidences.
    9. Avez-vous de petits cahiers?
    10. Ce sont de mauvais journaux.

D. 1. J'ai plusieurs examens.
    2. Voilà un groupe d'étudiantes.
    3. Avez-vous assez d'argent?
    4. Nous mangeons beaucoup de moules.
    5. Il a peu de cheveux blancs.

    6. Il veut un carnet de tickets.
    7. J'ai un peu de temps.
    8. Je voudrais un kilo de bœuf.
    9. Combien de vin as-tu?
    10. Elle commande un paquet de cigarettes.

E. 1. Ce sont des exercices oraux.
    2. Elle adore les petits animaux.
    3. Leurs amis sont loyaux.
    4. Voici les détails finals.
    5. Les tableaux sont originaux.

    6. Les généraux travaillent aux hôpitaux.
    7. Ce sont des prix spéciaux.
    8. Où sont les thèmes principaux?
    9. Nous admirons ses travaux.
    10. Voilà des étudiants orientaux.

F. 1. voulons
    2. Veux
    3. veulent
    4. Voulez
    5. veut

    6. veux
    7. veulent
    8. veut
    9. veut
    10. voulons

G. 1. Je voudrais du bœuf, des petits pois et du vin pour mon dîner.
    2. Elle veut sortir mais elle a trop de travail.
    3. Combien d'examens finals as-tu?
    4. Avez-vous de vieux journaux?
    5. Ils n'aiment pas la glace; ils veulent du fruit et du fromage pour le dessert.
    6. Veut-il emprunter une paire de jeans et une paire de chaussures?
    7. Est-ce que Paul n'a pas d'argent à prêter?
    8. Voudriez-vous une tasse de café? --Non, merci...un verre d'eau, s'il vous plaît.
    9. On sert du poisson ici--du bon poisson.
    10. Tu as autant de disques que Philippe.

I.

A.

II.
A.
1. réponds
2. rompt
3. descendez
4. mord
5. bats

6. Perdez
7. vendent
8. rendons
9. Entends
10. attendent

B.
1. La/la
2. Le
3. La/l'
4. Le
5. Le

6. Le
7. Les/la
8. La/la
9. La/le
10. le

C.
1. ...il va en Angleterre.
2. ...ils vont aux Etats-Unis.
3. ...je vais en Espagne.
4. ...tu vas en Egypte.
5. ...nous allons au Canada.

6. ...il va en France.
7. ...on va en Belgique.
8. ...vous allez en Italie.
9. ...ils vont au Mexique.
10. ...je vais au Brésil.

D.
1. On téléphone du Portugal.
2. On téléphone de Suède.
3. On téléphone du Japon.
4. On téléphone de Chine.
5. On téléphone d'Italie.

6. On téléphone du Québec.
7. On téléphone de France.
8. On téléphone d'Australie.
9. On téléphone d'Angleterre.
10. On téléphone des Pays-Bas/
   de Hollande.

E. 1. Ne les as-tu pas?   6. Il ne le demande pas.
    2. Elle nous regarde.   7. Le cherche-t-elle?
    3. La voici.   8. Les voilà.
    4. Nous allons les attendre ici.   9. Vous le commandez.
    5. Pourquoi l'écoutes-tu?   10. Tu ne veux pas la payer.

F. 1. Nous allons voyager.   6. Georges ne va pas marcher en ville.
    2. On va obéir au professeur.   7. Je vais téléphoner à Paris.
    3. Tu ne vas pas partir demain.   8. Tout le monde va travailler.
    4. Ils vont préparer le repas.   9. Les jeunes filles vont sortir
    5. Vous allez passer l'examen.   avec les garçons.
                                            10. Tu ne vas pas aller en Suisse.

G. 1. Les étudiants ne vont pas m'attendre.
    2. Voilà une nouvelle voiture. Je veux la regarder.
    3. Elle va en Europe parce qu'elle va étudier à Paris.
    4. Pourquoi cherches-tu ton livre? Je l'ai.
    5. Voici un étudiant du Japon.
    6. Voulez-vous vendre vos disques? Je les veux.
    7. Il va téléphoner à ses parents de Varsovie.
    8. Je n'aime pas les Etats-Unis et je ne veux pas les visiter.
    9. Ils vont passer leurs vacances en Espagne.
   10. Quand va-t-elle revenir de Chicago?

Chapitre Sept

I.
A. 1. passer/échouer à/rater/préparer/réussir à
    2. poser/répondre à

B. 1. savoureux   5. sec
    2. sportif   6. studieux/sérieux
    3. amoureux   7. blanc
    4. malheureux   8. faux

II.
A. 1. Il nous téléphone.   6. Il va vous parler.
    2. Je leur donne mon numéro de   7. Nous voulons leur rendre visite.
       téléphone.   8. Les enfants leur ressemblent.
    3. Lui obéissez-vous?   9. Ils lui prêtent un dollar.
    4. Ils leur demandent d'entrer.   10. Elle lui emprunte des vêtements.
    5. Lui réponds-tu?

B. 1. Attendez.   6. Ayez de la patience.
    2. Allez à droite.   7. Finis ton travail.
    3. Ouvre la fenêtre.   8. Va à la poste.
    4. Répondez à la question.   9. Téléphonez souvent.
    5. Sois sage.   10. Tournez à gauche.

C. 1. Préparez-le.   6. Attendez-le.
    2. Téléphonez-leur.   7. Ne les perdez pas.
    3. Ne le ratez pas.   8. Cherchez-le.
    4. Ne lui pardonnez pas.   9. Parlez-moi.
    5. Choisissez-les.   10. Ne le décrochez pas.

D.

```
D A N G E R E U S E
O H R R N S G E L V
U B V E M E U F I
C R U C L A S G E T
E V H Q P T S N V C
E S U E R U O M A
E S U E S A L C F
E H C N A R F Q U D
M L S P O R T I V E
E H C N A L B C V L
H E U R E U S E H E
```

E. 1. obtiens
    2. reviennent
    3. appartiens
    4. venons
    5. devient
    6. tenez
    7. vient
    8. revenez
    9. appartiennent
   10. obtiens

F. 1. Je viens de finir mon travail.
    2. Elle vient de partir.
    3. Nous venons de passer un examen.
    4. Ils viennent de sortir de la salle.
    5. Vous venez de commander votre repas.
    6. On vient de vous demander.
    7. Tu viens d'arriver.
    8. Les hommes viennent de descendre du train.
    9. Nous venons d'accepter une invitation.
   10. Je viens de nager dans la piscine.

G. 1. Tu ressembles à ton père. Est-ce que ta sœur lui ressemble aussi?
    2. Les motocyclettes sont dangereuses.
    3. Téléphonez-moi demain; ne me téléphonez pas aujourd'hui.
    4. Elle vient de lui donner son cahier.
    5. Si un agent de police vous arrête, allez-vous lui obéir?
    6. Ayons une longue conversation sérieuse.
    7. Je viens de manger, donc ne m'offrez pas de nourriture.
    8. Mes enfants, soyez sages. Ne téléphonez pas à votre père.
    9. Nous venons d'aller à la gare pour te chercher.
   10. Elle va devenir professeur.

Chapitre Huit

I. 1. la cuisine
    2. la chambre
    3. le garage
    4. la salle de bains
    5. les W.C./la toilette
    6. le réfrigérateur/le frigo
    7. le placard
    8. la salle de séjour/ le living-room
    9. le mur
   10. le rez-de-chaussée

II.
A. 1. Il les leur rend.
2. Nous ne la lui demandons pas.
3. Elle la lui prête.
4. Vous nous les vendez.
5. Ils veulent les leur montrer.

6. Tu le lui empruntes.
7. Je le lui commande.
8. Il ne les leur pardonne pas.
9. Elle va le leur laisser.
10. Nous le leur apprenons.

B. 1. Ne les lui donnez pas.
2. Ne la leur vendons pas.
3. Ne me les montrez pas.
4. Ne nous le prête pas.
5. Ne la lui rendez pas.

6. Ne me la passe pas.
7. Ne nous les raconte pas.
8. Ne le lui prends pas.
9. Ne les leur empruntons pas.
10. Ne me le demande pas.

C. 1. Elle porte une blouse parisienne.
2. J'aime l'eau fraîche.
3. Tu veux de grosses pommes.
4. On trouve des montagnes basses.
5. Nous détestons les plantes artificielles.

6. Vous n'aimez pas les personnes indiscrètes.
7. C'est ma dernière classe.
8. C'est ma chère amie.
9. Ils vont à une plage secrète.
10. Il a une gentille femme.

D. 1. 2093
2. 71
3. 1002
4. 47
5. 919

6. 555
7. 32
8. 1492
9. 66
10. 100

E. 1. apprennent
2. Comprends
3. prenez
4. surprend
5. apprends

6. prenons
7. prend
8. comprend
9. apprennent
10. surprenez

F. 1. Je veux regarder ton livre. Montre-le-moi, s'il te plaît.
2. Elle prend une douche encore.
3. J'ai de vielles photos et je vais vous les donner.
4. Elle n'est pas très discrète, donc ne le lui dites pas.
5. Habitez-vous une maison particulière ou un immeuble?
6. Il y a quatre-vingt-six étudiants dans ma classe de biologie.
7. Est-ce que votre maison est très chère? --C'est une question très indiscrète!
8. Ils ont vingt-deux pièces dans leur maison.
9. Déjeunez-vous ici à l'école?
10. Si vous voulez l'adresse de Jacques, demandez-la-lui!

Chapitre Neuf

I.
A. 1. hier
2. décembre
3. l'été
4. l'heure
5. l'après-midi

6. l'hiver
7. juin, juillet, août
8. une semaine
9. lundi
10. d'habitude

B. 1. Il pleut.
    2. Il fait frais.
    3. Il neige/Il fait froid.
    4. Le ciel est couvert.
    5. Il fait du vent.
    6. Il gèle.
    7. Il fait mauvais.
    8. Il fait (très) chaud.

C. 1. le footing
    2. le hockey
    3. la natation
    4. le basketball
    5. le baseball
    6. le ski
    7. le tennis
    8. le football/le hockey

II. A.
1. a. Il est quatre heures moins le quart du matin.
    b. Il est trois heures quarante-cinq.
2. a. Il est dix heures et demie du soir.
    b. Il est vingt-deux heures trente.
3. a. Il est trois heures moins dix de l'après-midi.
    b. Il est quatroze heures cinquante.
4. a. Il est quatre heures et quart du matin.
    b. Il est quatre heures quinze.
5. a. Il est midi et demi.
    b. Il est douze heures trente.
6. a. Il est une heure moins cinq du matin.
    b. Il est zéro heure cinquante-cinq.
7. a. Il est neuf heures du matin.
    b. Il est neuf heures.
8. a. Il est deux heures moins vingt de l'après-midi.
    b. Il est treize heures quarante.

B. 1. août
    2. mercredi
    3. jour
    4. après-midi
    5. printemps
    6. aujourd'hui
    7. avril
    8. dimanche

C.

D. 1. Elle a dîné avec ses amis.
2. Nous avons répondu aux questions.
3. J'ai dormi huit heures.
4. Ils ont vendu leur voiture.
5. Il a servi le repas.
6. Vous avez commandé un café.
7. J'ai eu du travail.
8. Il a été à la plage.
9. J'ai ouvert la porte.
10. Ils ont entendu de la musique.

E. 1. Oui, il l'a regardée.
2. Oui, je les ai faits.
3. Oui, je l'ai finie.
4. Oui, il l'a fermée.
5. Oui, elle les a servies.
6. Oui, je les ai mangées.
7. Oui, ils l'ont choisie.
8. Oui, je les ai visités.
9. Oui, elle les a perdus.
10. Oui, je l'ai posée.

F. 1. fait
2. fais
3. font
4. faisons
5. Fais
6. faites
7. fait
8. fait
9. faisons
10. faites

G. 1. Allez-vous faire des achats demain?
2. J'ai fait du jogging à six heures et demie du matin.
3. Elle a fait la tarte. L'avez-vous aimée?
4. Nous avons passé la journée à la plage samedi.
5. Nous allons à l'église d'habitude le dimanche.
6. Où sont les chassures que vous avez trouvées? --Pourquoi, les avez-vous perdues?
7. L'émission a commencé à huit heures et demie du soir. L'avez-vous regardée?
8. Elle a fait ses valises, a téléphoné à son ami(e) et a pris le train en Floride.
9. Avez-vous eu le temps d'étudier mes notes? - Oui, je les ai étudiées.
10. Quel temps fait-il aujourd'hui? --Il fait du soleil mais il fait du vent.

Chapitre Dix

I.

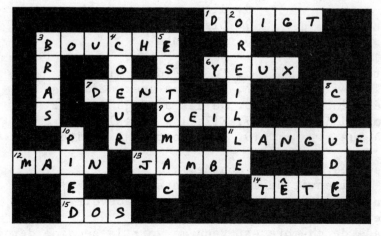

II.

A. Descendre   Venir
    Revenir   Aller
       &   Naître
    Montrer   Devenir
    Rentrer   Entrer
    Sortir   Retourner
                   Tomber
                   Rester
                   Arriver
                   Mourir
                   Partir

B. 1. Nous sommes allés chez le médecin.
    2. Elle est retournée à l'école après deux heures.
    3. Vous êtes descendu de l'avion.
    4. Elles sont tombées dans la neige.
    5. Il n'est pas revenu de son voyage.
    6. Tu es entrée dans l'immeuble.
    7. Ils sont devenus malades.
    8. La pauvre femme est-elle morte?
    9. Les garçons ne sont pas partis de la gare.
   10. Je suis resté(e) au lit.

C. 1. Le pauvre garçon   5. une ville ancienne
    2. dernière classe   6. mon propre travail
    3. votre cher ami   7. Le soldat brave
    4. le même jour   8. une certaine faveur

D. 1. Il a envie de danser.   6. Elle a honte.
    2. Nous avons faim.   7. Philippe a rendez-vous
    3. Le concert a lieu ce soir.   avec toi.
    4. Vous avez tort.   8. Ils ont soif.
    5. J'ai mal aux dents.   9. Nous avons besoin d'argent.
    5. J'ai mal aux dents.   10. Il a dix-neuf ans.

E. 1. Ecris   6. dit
    2. dites   7. écrivons
    3. lisent   8. dit
    4. écris   9. Lisez
    5. Lisez   10. écrivent

F. 1. Elle l'a déjà écrite.   6. Tu l'as déjà dite.
    2. Je l'ai déjà dit.   7. Vous les avez déjà lus.
    3. Le médecin l'a déjà écrite. 8. Je les ai déjà écrits.
    4. Les étudiants l'ont déjà écrit. 9. Elle l'a déjà lu.
    5. Nous l'avons déjà lue.   10. Ils l'ont déjà écrite.

G. 1. Quand elle est rentrée, elle est montée.
    2. Avez-vous faim? J'ai envie de manger maintenant.
    3. Nous avons besoin d'un crayon pour écrire notre devoir.
    4. Il a dit qu'il ne lui a pas encore écrit.
    5. Mon ancien camarade de chambre est venu me voir la semaine dernière.
    6. Christophe lui a dit de fermer les yeux.

7. J'ai descendu la valise pour ma mère.
8. La pauvre femme! Son mari est mort.
9. Elle a vingt-deux ans, et elle est née au Canada.
10. Dites-moi si Michel a raison ou s'il a tort.

Chapitre Onze

I.

The crossword grid contains:
- 1 (down) F I L L E
- 2 (across) F I L S
- 3 (down) G R A N D M è r E
- 4 (across) P A R E N T
- 5 (across) P È R E
- 6 (across) N E V E U
- 7 (down) E N F A N T
- 8 (down) T A N T E
- 9 (down) S O E U R
- 10 (across) N I È C E
- 11 (across) O N C L E
- F R è R E (down)

II.

A.
1. elle
2. moi
3. eux
4. vous
5. toi
6. elles
7. moi
8. lui
9. moi
10. elles

B.
1. Ils veulent te parler, eux.
2. Tu as tort, toi.
3. Il m'a écrit, lui.
4. Nous ne savons pas, nous.
5. Je vais le faire, moi.
6. Il est tombé de sa bicyclette, lui.
7. Vous le lui avez dit, vous?
8. Ils ne comprennent pas la question, eux.

C.
1. Avais-tu mal à la tête?
2. Ils savaient la réponse.
3. J'étais ici.
4. Nous faisions nos devoirs.
5. Allait-il à l'église?
6. Elle finissait son dîner.
7. Elles prenaient le métro.
8. Je venais vous rendre visite.
9. On lisait en français.
10. Tu m'attendais?

D.
1. Ils allaient au cinéma le samedi.
2. Il était 3h30.
3. Nous voulions partir.
4. Je n'avais pas d'argent.
5. Elle savait le nom du garçon.
6. Il faisait froid hier.
7. Nous apprenions le français.
8. Tu n'aimais pas le voyage.
9. Il neigeait dans les montagnes.
10. Elle avait sommeil.

E. étais/était/lisais/ai regardé/ai entendu/avait/est sorti/avait/
   est allé/a donné/est entré/ai téléphoné/est arrivée/a arrêté/
   sont rentrés/ai quitté/ai raconté/étaient/m'ont invité

F. 1. savons   6. sait
   2. sais   7. sais
   3. savent   8. Sait
   4. Sais   9. sait
   5. savez   10. savent

G. 1. Je savais faire du ski.
   2. Elle ne l'a pas fait; lui l'a fait!
   3. Quand je suis rentré(e), il était deux heures du matin.
   4. Quand son petit ami téléphonait, ils parlaient longtemps.
   5. Ils savaient qu'elle n'allait pas accepter leur invitation.
   6. Christophe et moi, nous faisons un voyage en Europe.
   7. Je regrette, mais mon père dit que je ne sors pas avec toi.
   8. Il faisait très mauvais hier et j'étais enrhumé(e).
   9. Il nous a donné, à Michel et à moi, cinq dollars.
   10. Elle a su qu'il sortait avec une autre jeune fille.

Chapitre Douze

I.
A. 1. se laver/se brosser/   6. se souvenir de/se rappeler
      se peigner/se sécher   7. s'appeler
   2. se brosser   8. se lever/se réveiller
   3. s'endormir   9. s'arrêter
   4. se mettre à   10. se tromper (de)
   5. se dépêcher

B.

C. 1. d'abord   4. d'habitude
   2. aujourd'hui   5. jamais
   3. avant   6. tôt

II.

A.
1. nous levons
2. t'arrêtes
3. vous rendez
4. se maquille
5. se fâchent
6. m'en vais
7. se débrouillent
8. nous habillons
9. te souviens
10. vous écrivez

B.
1. Te brosses-tu les dents?
2. Vous amusez-vous avec elle?
3. Anne s'endort-elle en classe?
4. Nous intéressons-nous à cela?
5. Se téléphonent-ils souvent?
6. Comment se sent-elle?
7. Les jeunes filles se rencontrent-elles après la classe?
8. Vous rasez-vous la moustache?
9. T'habilles-tu élégamment?
10. Se souvient-il de cela?

C.
1. Il ne s'est pas demandé pourquoi.
2. Elle s'est amusée en vacances.
3. Tu t'es couché(e) de bonne heure.
4. Nous nous sommes occupés de cela.
5. Ils ne se sont pas parlé.
6. Paul et Marie se sont mariés.
7. Je me suis baigné(e) dans la mer.
8. Elles se sont dépêchées.
9. Il s'est rasé la barbe.
10. Ils se sont dit salut.

D.
1. Elle veut se maquiller.
2. Nous voulons nous rencontrer.
3. Ils veulent se saluer.
4. Je veux me laver.
5. Tu veux te laver.
6. Vous voulez vous en aller.
7. Il veut se tromper.
8. Elles veulent se téléphoner.
9. Je veux me coucher.
10. Nous voulons nous endormir.

E.
1. également
2. fréquemment
3. continuellement
4. malheureusement
5. simplement
6. méchamment
7. actuellement
8. couramment
9. sportivement
10. franchement

F.
1. Ils sont partis hier.
2. J'ai déjà passé l'examen.
3. Elle parle couramment le russe.
4. Nous allions souvent à la plage.
5. T'es-tu levé tôt ce matin?
6. Il a activement participé.
7. Je sais bien la réponse.
8. Ils s'en sont allés enfin.
9. Elle m'a téléphoné immédiatement.
10. Paul est toujours en France.

G.
1. Il étudie le français depuis trois ans.
2. Il y a trois mois que je suis ici.
3. Voilà un an que nous travaillons à Paris.
4. Il cherche son livre depuis deux semaines.
5. Voilà plusieurs jours qu'elle est malade.

6. Il y a cinq heures que je regarde la télévision.
7. Je t'attends depuis quinze minutes.
8. Vous habitez ici depuis dix ans.
9. Voilà une demi-heure qu'il se lave.
10. Il y a huit jours que je lis ce livre.

H. 1. Voilà (Il y a) trois heures que j'attends Philippe./
   J'attends Philippe depuis trois heures.
2. Il a vite fait ses devoirs et s'est couché.
3. Quand nous nous sommes vu(e)s, nous nous sommes dit bonjour et
   nous nous sommes serré la main.
4. Depuis combien de temps êtes-vous étudiant ici? --Je suis
   étudiant depuis deux ans.
5. Elle s'est levée lentement, s'est regardée et s'est maquillée.
6. Nous dînons depuis une heure et demie.
7. Ils (Elles) ne se sont pas écrit fréquemment.
8. Depuis combien de temps voulez-vous sortir avec lui?
9. Elle s'est fâchée quand je lui ai dit de se peigner les cheveux.
10. Nous nous sommes mis au travail d'abord, mais nous nous sommes
    reposés longtemps.

Chapitre Treize

I. 1. Les bagages
   2. le guichet
   3. la consigne
   4. le kiosque
   5. le buffet
   6. la salle d'attente
   7. la couchette
   8. un (billet) aller et retour
   9. le supplément
   10. un (billet) simple

II.
A. 1. Pourquoi y allez-vous?
   2. Combien de temps allez-vous
      y rester?
   3. Quand partez-vous?
   4. Comment y allez-vous?
   5. D'où partez-vous?
   6. Où allez-vous étudier?
   7. Combien de cours allez-vous
      suivre?
   8. Pourquoi avez-vous choisi
      l'Institut?
   9. Quand revenez-vous?
   10. Comment allez-vous voyager?

B. 1. Comment Paul parle-t-il
      français?
   2. Quand part Marie?
   3. Combien de devoirs ont les
      garçons?
   4. Pourquoi Luc y va-t-il?
   5. Où est le professeur?
   6. D'où reviennent les étudiants?
   7. Quand est-ce que Philippe est né?
   8. Où arrivent les touristes?
   9. Pourquoi Lucille ne vient-elle pas?
   10. Combien de frères a Anne?

C. 1. Elle y a répondu.
   2. Ils y sont arrivés à l'heure.
   3. Y penses-tu?
   4. J'y ai trouvé l'article.
   5. Nous nous y intéressons.
   6. Je ne veux pas y voyager.
   7. Vas-y maintenant!
   8. Ils y allaient le dimanche.
   9. Vous y êtes-vous baigné?
   10. N'y as-tu pas fait attention?

D. 1. Qu'en pense-t-il?
2. Ils en sont revenus.
3. N'en avez-vous pas besoin?
4. Elle en a trois.
5. Je m'en occupe.
6. Nous ne voulons pas nous en passer.
7. Parle-lui-en!
8. Il y en a beaucoup à notre université.
9. Il m'en a téléphoné.
10. Tu n'en manges pas?

E. 1. C'est une femme qui habite chez moi.
2. Voilà l'avion qui arrive maintenant.
3. Je parle à M. Dupont qui est mon professeur.
4. Christophe, qui est mon camarade de chambre, a une sœur.
5. Nous avons vu un film qui était intéressant.
6. Elle vient d'acheter une voiture qui coûte cher.
7. J'ai préparé la leçon qui est très longue.
8. Vous avez fait la connaissance de Michel qui est mon cousin.
9. Ils ont choisi une école qui est dans le nord.
10. Il est sorti avec Anne qui est charmante.

F. 1. As-tu le livre que je cherchais?
2. C'est un homme qu'il demande depuis une heure.
3. Nous étudions une composition qu'elle a écrite.
4. Voici les vêtements qu'elle a portés hier.
5. Jean-Pierre a un voisin que je n'aime pas du tout.
6. Où est la place qu tu as choisie?
7. Avez-vous vu l'addition que Paul a déjà payée?
8. La dame que vous voyez là-bas a 80 ans.
9. C'est un pays que je voudrais visiter.
10. C'est un avocat que tout le monde respecte.

G. 1. voit
2. Vois
3. voient
4. Voyez
5. vois
6. voit
7. voyons
8. voit
9. voit
10. Voient

H. 1. Nous avons vu la jeune fille que vous cherchiez.
2. Avez-vous un stylo? --Non, je n'en ai pas. Pourquoi? En avez-vous besoin?
3. J'y ai pensé longtemps.
4. Elle vient de me donner le livre que je voulais.
5. Pourquoi voulez-vous aller en France? --J'ai des amis qui y étudient.
6. Combien de plantes avez-vous? --J'en ai seize.
7. D'où partait Guy?
8. Avez-vous jamais vu un film qui vous a rendu(e) triste?
9. Si vous ne trouvez pas le disque de musique française que vous voulez, j'en ai un.
10. Quand le téléphone a sonné, j'y ai répondu.

I.

A.
1. balayer
2. essuyer
3. essayer
4. effrayer
5. employer
6. s'ennuyer
7. nettoyer
8. envoyer

B.
1. acheter
2. enlever
3. se promener
4. s'appeler
5. rejeter
6. corriger
7. partager
8. voyager
9. répéter
10. ranger

II.

A.
1. aurons
2. ira
3. attendrai
4. Feras
5. Verrez
6. finira
7. appellera
8. saurai
9. parleront
10. voudrez

B.
1. seras/partirons
2. se lèveront/iront
3. dînera/reviendront
4. ferez/finira
5. voudras/verras

D.

E. 1. Puis
    2. peux
    3. peuvent
    4. Pouvez
    5. peux
    6. pouvons
    7. peut
    8. peuvent
    9. Peut
    10. peux

F. 1. Vous paierez votre chemise à la caisse.
    2. Ils ne pourront pas essayer de vêtements parce qu'ils ne savent pas leurs tailles.
    3. Comment vous appelez-vous? --Je m'appelle Jean-Pierre Lahon.
    4. Si Denis veut le voir, il téléphonera pour un rendez-vous.
    5. Quand j'arriverai en France, j'irai d'abord à mon hôtel pour me reposer.
    6. Combien pesez-vous? --Je pèse cinquante-cinq kilos.
    7. Dès que (Aussitôt que) vous achèterez votre voiture, me la montrerez-vous?
    8. Ne dérange pas ton frère; il se lèvera bientôt.
    9. Je n'ai pas pu aller à la boum. Nous nettoyions notre chambre.
    10. Quand nous corrigeons nos phrases, le professeur les répète toujours.

Chapitre Quinze

I. 1. toucher
    2. un billet
    3. de la petite monnaie
    4. le cours
    5. de la monnaie
    6. le caissier
    7. un chèque de voyage
    8. le bureau de change

II.
A. 1. Qu'est-ce qui fait ce bruit?
    2. Qui l'a écrit?
    3. Qu'est-ce qui ne marche pas bien?
    4. Qui vous en a prêté?
    5. Qui viendra à midi?
    6. Qu'est-ce qui le rend malade?
    7. Qui parle chinois?
    8. Qui m'appellera?
    9. Qu'est-ce qui partira dans dix minutes?
    10. Qui va leur téléphoner?

B. 1. Qui avez-vous vu?/ Qui est-ce que vous avez vu?
    2. Qui connaissait-elle?/ Qui est-ce qu'elle connaissait?
    3. Qui avez-vous payé?/ Qui est-ce que vous avez payé?
    4. Qui est-ce que j'ai accompagné?
    5. Qui Henri a-t-il salué?/ Qui est-ce qu'Henri a salué?
    6. Qui y amènera-t-elle?/Qui est-ce qu'elle y amènera?
    7. Qui veut-il regarder?/ Qui est-ce qu'il veut regarder?
    8. Qui choisissez-vous?/ Qui est-ce que vous choisissez?
    9. Qui ont-ils puni?/ Qui est-ce qu'ils ont puni?
    10. Qui attendras-tu au buffet?/ Qui est-ce que tu attendras au buffet?

C. 1. Qu'est-ce que
    2. Qu'est-ce qu'
    3. Que
    4. Que
    5. Qu'est-ce qu'
    6. Qu'est-ce que
    7. Que
    8. Que
    9. Qu'est-ce que
    10. Que

D. 1. cette
   2. cet
   3. Ces
   4. ce
   5. cette

   6. Cette
   7. ces
   8. Cet
   9. ces
   10. ce

E. 1. connais
   2. connaît
   3. connaissons
   4. connais
   5. connaissez

   6. connaissent
   7. connaît
   8. connaissons
   9. connaît
   10. connais

F. 1. sais
   2. Sais
   3. connaissons
   4. connaît
   5. Savez

   6. Savent
   7. connais
   8. sait
   9. Savez
   10. connaissons

G. 1. Savez-vous le cours aujourd'hui?
   2. Cet homme que vous voyez là-bas est le caissier. Ne le
      saviez-vous pas?
   3. Cette banque-ci est nouvelle; cette banque-là est très vieille.
   4. Je savais parler français.
   5. Voici les livres qu'elle m'a apportés hier.
   6. Qu'est-ce qui se passe ici? Qui est cet homme?
   7. Avez-vous plus de ces pulls?
   8. Elle a perdu ses chèques de voyage. Savez-vous où ils sont?
   9. Qui est sa petite amie? --Cette jeune fille-là!
   10. Qui avez-vous vu à cette boum? En connaissiez-vous beaucoup?

Chapitre Seize

I.
B. 1. –
   2. +
   3. +
   4. –

   5. +
   6. –
   7. +
   8. +

II.
B. 1. Anne est la moins grande.
   2. C'est la plus petite voiture.
   3. Il est resté le plus longtemps.
   4. Ils écrivent la moins longue lettre.
   5. J'ai les livres les plus chers.
   6. C'est le plus beau timbre.
   7. Vous arrivez le plus tard en classe.
   8. Je le voyais le moins souvent.
   9. Il a commandé le repas le plus délicieux.
   10. Elle a les yeux les plus bleus.

C. 1. Le film était meilleur.
      L'émission était la meilleure.
   2. Je parle mieux le français.
      Tu parles le mieux le français.
   3. Vous avez plus de travail.
      Paul a le plus de travail.
   4. Les desserts sont plus mauvais.
      Les boissons sont les plus mauvaises.
   5. Ton ami chante plus mal.
      Elle chante le plus mal.
   6. Tu te sens mieux.
      Le professeur se sent le mieux.

D.

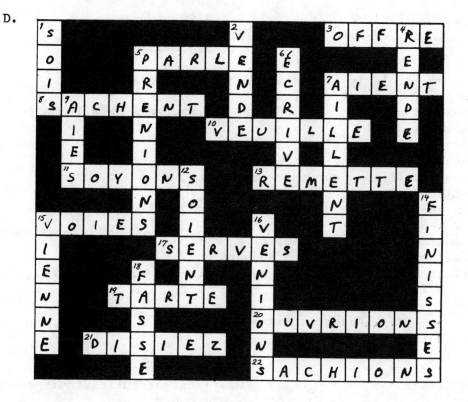

E. 1. J'ai peur qu'il ne vienne pas.
   2. Il est amusant que tu dises cela.
   3. Je suis heureux qu'elle aime mon cadeau.
   4. Il est bon que vous étudiiez le français.
   5. Il est absurde qu'ils ne le sachent pas.
   6. Je regrette qu'il ne veuille pas me voir.
   7. C'est dommage que tu ne puisses pas y aller.
   8. Il est étrange qu'elle se fâche contre toi.
   9. Je suis surpris qu'il lise ma lettre.
   10. Il est extraordinaire que vous ne compreniez pas.

F. 1. Je veux vous aider.
   2. Je veux que vous m'aidiez.
   3. Notre professeur ne permet pas que nous parlions pendant un examen./Notre professeur ne nous permet pas de parler pendant un examen.
   4. Elle souhaite qu'il parte.
   5. Ils détestent que vous disiez cela.
   6. Me permettrez-vous de sortir?/Permettrez-vous que je sorte?
   7. Elle préfère manger seul.
   8. Il a ordonné qu'ils paient./Il leur a ordonné de payer.

G. 1. admets   6. mettez
   2. mettent   7. promets
   3. promets   8. permettent
   4. mettons   9. mets
   5. commet   10. admettons

H. 1. C'est la jeune fille la plus sympathique de la classe.
   2. J'ai plus de timbres que vous.
   3. Elle ne se sent pas bien aujourd'hui. Je regrette qu'elle ne se sente pas mieux.
   4. Il est plus facile de parler que d'écrire.
   5. Vouliez-vous qu'il prenne le plus grand morceau de gâteau?
   6. Est-il plus intelligent que sa sœur? --Non, elle est aussi intelligente que lui.
   7. C'est dommage qu'elle ne soit pas si (aussi) belle que sa camarade de chambre.
   8. Il a mis ses meilleures chaussures.
   9. Nous sommes contents d'être ici aujourd'hui.
  10. Me promettrez-vous de travailler aussi fort que vous pouvez?

Chapitre Six-Sept

I.
A. 1. il faut   5. il est incertain
   2. il est important   6. il est essentiel/indispensable
   3. il se peut   7. je doute
   4. il est impossible   8. il est temps

B. 1. en centimètres   5. en mètres
   2. en kilogrammes   6. en centilitres
   3. en kilomètres   7. en mètres
   4. en litres   8. en centimètres

II.
A. 1. Je doute que nous ayons un examen dans dix minutes.
   2. Je doute que le professeur ait 89 ans.
   3. Je doute qu'on vienne en classe demain.
   4. Je doute qu mon voisin/ma voisine comprenne la leçon.
   5. Je doute qu'il neige demain.
   6. Je doute qu'il y ait une autre guerre.
   7. Je doute qu'on habite sur la lune.

8. Je doute que vous me donniez 1000F.
9. Je doute que Paul connaisse le Président.
10. Je doute que mon ami reste cinq ans à l'université.

B. 1. Il est essentiel que Jean-Pierre vienne immédiatement.
2. Il est bon que nous célébrions aujourd'hui.
3. Il est important que vous lui achetiez un cadeau.
4. Il vaut mieux qu'elle me téléphone maintenant.
5. Il est just que je choisisse mes cours.
6. Il est temps qu'ils aillent à la bibliothèque.
7. Il suffit que tu m'écrives souvent.
8. Il est indispensable que je sois ici à l'heure.
9. Il est recommandé qu'elle sache parler français.
10. Il faut que nous partions plus tard.

C. 1. cent unième 101e 6. cinquième 5^e
2. neuvième 9e 7. quatre-vingt-deuxième 82^e
3. seizième 16e 8. deuxième 2e/second(e) 2^e
4. quarante-cinquième 45e 9. quatre-vingt-dix-neuvième 99^e
5. soixante et onzième 71e 10. premier/première 1er/1ère

D. 1. un quart   5. trois quarts
2. deux tiers   6. cinq huitièmes
3. neuf dixièmes   7. un tiers
4. un demi   8. quatre septièmes

E. 1. le seize décembre mille neuf cent trente-neuf
2. le dix-sept octobre mille neuf cent soixante-huit
3. le vingt mai mille neuf cent quarante
4. le premier janvier mille neuf cent quatre-vingt-quatre
5. le vingt-neuf septembre mille neuf cent cinquante-cinq

F. 1. crois   6. croit
2. croyez   7. croit
3. croyons   8. croient
4. crois   9. croient
5. croit   10. crois

G. 1. Je ne suis pas sûr(e) qu'il puisse vous aider beaucoup.
2. Il est temps que nous partions maintenant.
3. Elle ne croit pas que ce soit le premier du mois!
4. Est-il possible qu'il puisse manger deux tiers de ce gâteau?
5. Est-il juste que vous lui permettiez d'y aller?
6. Il faut que je prépare ma leçon ce soir.
7. Ne croyez-vous pas qu'elle soit belle?
8. Combien de femmes Henri VIII (huit) a-t-il eues?
9. Je suis sûr(e) qu'il vous téléphonera demain.
10. Il est bon que vous étudiiez une autre langue.

I.

A.
1. jamais
2. personne
3. plus
4. rien
5. jamais
6. guère
7. guère

B.
1. l'essai
2. l'histoire/le conte
3. l'écrivain
4. la pièce/la scène/l'acte
5. le roman, l'écrivain
6. le paragraphe
7. la pièce
8. le discours
9. la poésie, le poète, le poème

II.

A.

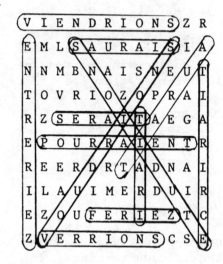

B.
1. Il a dit que nous pourrions venir.
2. Il a dit que tu mangerais beaucoup.
3. Il a dit que je serais surpris.
4. Il a dit qu'elle l'accompagnerait.
5. Il a dit que tout le monde voudrait participer.
6. Il a dit qu'ils viendraient nous chercher.
7. Il a dit que vous feriez attention.
8. Il a dit que nous verrions beaucoup d'amis.
9. Il a dit que j'enverrais une invitation.
10. Il a dit qu'il me téléphonerait ce soir.

C.
1. Si Assurancetourix chantait mieux, tout le monde l'écouterait.
2. Si Obélix était plus fort, les Romains en auraient peur.
3. Si vous preniez la potion magique de Panoramix, vous deviendriez surhumain.
4. Si les Bretons n'etaient pas gentils, ils attaqueraient à 5h.
5. S'il y avait du thé, les Bretons en prendraient.
6. Si Obélix avait quelque chose à faire, il le ferait.
7. S'ils ne se connaissaient pas, ils ne se serraient pas la main.
8. Si ce n'était pas splendide, ce serait dommage.
9. Si on voulait du lait dans le thé, on en mettrait.
10. Si ce n'était pas l'heure, ils continueraient la bataille.

D. 1. Pourriez-vous me le dire?
   2. Je voudrais vous parler.
   3. Il aimerait te voir.
   4. Nous ne voudrions pas le faire.
   5. Ne pourriez-vous pas m'en
      prêter?
   6. Aimeriez-vous cette bière?
   7. Voudrait-il répéter la question?
   8. Pourrais-tu y aller?
   9. Est-ce que je pourrais vous
      montrer quelque chose?
   10. Que voudriez-vous manger?

E. 1. Elle n'a ni disques ni cassettes.
   2. Il n'est jamais en retard.
   3. Je n'ai vu personne dans ta chambre.
   4. Ils n'ont plus de travail.
   5. Personne ne vous a téléphoné.
   6. N'avez-vous pas le temps de me parler?
   7. Je n'ai guère de temps libre.
   8. Rien ne s'est passé en classe.
   9. Ni son père ni sa mère ne sont venus le voir.
   10. Tu ne lui écriras plus.

F. 1. Elle n'aime que le lait.
   2. Nous n'avons emprunté que trois dollars.
   3. Il ne parle qu'à son camarade de chambre.
   4. Ils n'ont acheté que des cartes postales.
   5. Tu ne passeras qu'un examen de chimie.
   6. Vous n'avez réussi qu'à un cours.
   7. Il ne sortait qu'avec Anne.
   8. Je ne lui ai écrit qu'une lettre.
   9. Nous n'avons eu qu'une voiture.
   10. Ils ne fument que des cigares.

G. 1. Conduit
   2. conduisons
   3. conduit
   4. conduisez
   5. conduis
   6. conduit
   7. conduis
   8. conduisent
   9. conduis
   10. conduisez

H. 1. Je n'ai plus d'argent. Pourriez-vous m'en prêter?
   2. Personne n'a traduit les phrases.
   3. Il conduisait ma voiture. S'il était prudent, je lui permettrais
      de la conduire encore.
   4. Elle n'a vu personne qu'elle connaissait à la boum.
   5. Ne voulez-vous plus jamais lui parler?
   6. Ni Michel ni Anne ne savent conduire ma voiture.
   7. Si je n'étais pas si occupée, je vous aiderais.
   8. Il ne mange que des hamburgers.
   9. Vous m'avez dit que vous me téléphoneriez, mais vous n'avez
      jamais téléphoné.
   10. Rien ne le surprendra!

I.

II.

A.
1. Elle ne connaît personne qui puisse l'aider.
2. Il me faut une route qui soit directe.
3. Nous avons besoin d'une voiture qui roule vite.
4. Paul cherche un ami qui soit sympathique.
5. Il n'y a rien qui le surprenne.
6. Vous cherchez une station-service qui ait de l'essence.
7. Il n'y a personne qui veuille le faire plus que lui.
8. Y a-t-il un autobus qui y aille sans s'arrêter?
9. Ils ont besoin d'une voiture qui soit spacieuse.
10. Il n'y a rien que vous puissiez dire.

B.
1. Je vous écrirai bien que je ne le veuille pas.
2. Il te prêtera de l'argent à moins que tu n'en aies pas besoin.
3. Nous vous inviterons pourvu que vous y ameniez votre copain.
4. Vous n'irez pas jusqu'à ce que je fasse le plein.
5. Il est allé à la plage sans que sa mère le sache.
6. Me téléphoneras-tu avant que je parte pour la boum?
7. Je ne lui parlerai pas de peur qu'il se fâche.
8. Il voudrait emprunter ta voiture afin que nous allions voir son frère.
9. Ils y viendront quoiqu'ils soient malades.
10. Je vous rejoindrai où que vous vous trouviez.

C. 1. Il s'est cassé le bras sans le savoir.
    2. Nous avons dîné avant de sortir ensemble.
    3. Je ferai le plein afin de pouvoir faire tout le voyage.
    4. Vous n'irez pas à moins de pouvoir nous accompagner.
    5. Je n'emprunterai pas sa voiture de peur d'avoir un accident.
    6. Elle lira la carte pour ne pas se perdre.
    7. Ils ne partiront pas de crainte de manquer un coup de téléphone.

D. 1. Il était possible qu'il soit parti.
       Maybe he had left.
    2. Je regrette que tu n'aies pas pu venir.
       I'm sorry you couldn't come.
    3. Il était bon qu'il en ait su la solution.
       It was good that he had known the solution.
    4. Nous doutons qu'ils aient compris.
       We doubt they understood.
    5. Avez-vous peur que nous soyons sortis sans vous?
       Are you afraid we left without you?
    6. Il est impossible qu'elle ait fait cela.
       It's impossible that she did that.
    7. Je cherchais un dictionnaire qui ait contenu tous les mots.
       I was looking for a dictionary which had all the words.
    8. Elle était contente que tu sois venue.
       She was happy that you had come.
    9. Il est nécessaire que vous ayez traduit la phrase.
       It is necessary for you to have translated the sentence.
    10. Tu doutes que j'aie fini avant midi?
       Do you doubt that I finished before noon?

E. 1. Il/C'   6. C'/C'
    2. C'   7. Ce
    3. c'   8. Il
    4. Il   9. Ils/ce
    5. Elle/Elle   10. Elle/C'

F. 1. reçois   6. reçoivent
    2. recevons   7. reçoit
    3. reçoit   8. reçoit
    4. Reçois   9. recevons
    5. recevez   10. reçoivent

G. 1. J'ai remarqué que la jeune fille vous a déçue. La connaissez-vous
       bien?
    2. Elle regrettait qu'il n'ait pas fait ses devoirs.
    3. Y a-t-il quelqu'un en classe qui sache parler plus d'une langue?
    4. Nous lui avons téléphoné pour qu'elle sache que nous pensions à elle.
    5. Ils vous écriront avant que vous partiez en vacances.
    6. C'est dommage qu'elle ait eu mal à l'estomac.
    7. Il est facile de recevoir de mauvaises notes! C'est vrai!
    8. Où est ma carte? Elle est sur la table.
    9. Elle ne conduira pas seule de peur de se perdre.
    10. Je resterai ici jusqu'à ce que vous reveniez.

I. 1. fiançailles   4. lune de miel
    2. cérémonie   5. mariage
    3. rapport

II.

A. 1. Ce sont eux derrière qui je marche.
    2. C'est M. Lahon pour qui il travaille.
    3. C'est lui sur qui nous comptons.
    4. C'est elle pour qui tu as voté.
    5. C'est Hélène à côté de qui il prend une place.
    6. C'est le professeur à qui vous parlez.
    7. C'est Guy en qui je n'ai pas confiance.
    8. C'est leur tante chez qui ils passeront les vacances.
    9. C'est le garçon sur qui il est tombé.
  10. C'est le médecin près de qui tu habites.

B. 1. C'est la piscine dans laquelle j'ai nagé.
    2. C'est le cinéma près duquel ma maison se trouve.
    3. C'est la table sous laquelle il a mis ses livres.
    4. C'est le marché auquel nous sommes allés.
    5. Ce sont ces pièces auxquelles tu as assisté.
    6. C'est cette raison pour laquelle j'ai écrit.
    7. C'est le fleuve le long duquel ils ont marché.
    8. C'est cette église dans laquelle ils se sont mariés.
    9. C'est la chaise sur laquelle vous avez laissé vos livres.
  10. Ce sont les villes loin desquelles elle veut habiter.

C. 1. Quels   6. quelle
    2. Quel   7. Quels
    3. Quel   8. quel
    4. Quelles   9. Quels
    5. Quel   10. Quelle

D. 1. devons   6. doit
    2. doit   7. dois
    3. Devez   8. doit
    4. dois   9. doivent
    5. doivent   10. devons

E. 1. Vous devez l'accompagner.   6. Nous avons dû assister au
    2. Vous devrez acheter un cadeau.   mariage.
    3. Nous devons le faire.   7. Elle a dû me le dire.
    4. Ils doivent se dépêcher.   8. Ils devront se marier.
    5. Je devrai parler au prêtre.   9. Il doit lui donner une bague.
                                   10. J'ai dû prendre un congé payé.

F. 1. Il devait quitter sa femme.   6. Tu dois arriver à midi.
    2. Nous devons le retrouver à 2h.   7. Je devais parler du divorce.
    3. Ils doivent partir en vacances.   8. On doit être à l'heure.
    4. Vous deviez me téléphoner.   9. Ils devaient passer leur lune de
    5. Anne devait assister au   miel à Londres.
        mariage.   10. Elle doivent chanter à la cérémon

G. 1. Tu devrais le savoir.
2. Je dois faire attention.
3. Vous devez l'y conduire.
4. Ils devraient leur permettre
d'y aller.
5. Nous devons nous en servir.

6. Il doit vouloir le faire.
7. Tu devrais accepter l'invitation.
8. Elle doit répondre à la lettre.
9. Ils doivent chercher une station-
service.
10. Vous devriez lire le poème.

H. 1. Qui est l'homme pour qui Michel travaille?
2. Voilà la chaise sur laquelle j'ai laissé mes livres. Où sont-ils?
Paul a dû les prendre.
3. Je devrais savoir la réponse à cette question. --Quelle
question?
4. Quel est le meilleur livre que vous avez lu l'année dernière?
5. Vous devriez faire la connaissance de l'homme à côté de qui elle
est assise.
6. Elle devait être ici à 9 heures du matin. Elle doit être ici
avant 10 heures!
7. L'homme à qui je parlais m'a demandé quel âge elle a.
8. Ne me devez-vous pas d'argent?
9. Je me rappellerai toujours l'église dans laquelle ils se sont
mariés.
10. Vous devez vous tromper!

Chapitre Vingt et un

I. 1. le médecin/l'infirmier
2. le juge/l'avocat
3. le menuisier/le plombier/
l'électricien

4. le comptable/la secrétaire
5. l'interprète
6. le technicien

II.
A. 1. De qui nous souvenons-nous?
2. Pour qui ont-ils voté?
3. Avec qui as-tu marché?
4. A qui est-ce que j'ai parlé?
5. A qui l'a-t-il demandé?

6. Avec qui s'est-elle mariée?
7. Devant qui étiez-vous?
8. Après qui sont-ils entrés?
9. Chez qui habiteras-tu?
10. A gauche de qui nous
trouverez-nous?

B. 1. De quoi as-tu besoin?
2. A quoi pensent-ils?
3. Contre quoi a-t-il parlé?
4. En face de quoi nous trouverons-nous?
5. Sur quoi est-ce que je compte?
6. Entre quoi faut-il choisir?
7. Dans quoi est-il entré?
8. Jusqu'à quoi marcherez-vous?
9. Au milieu de quoi se sont-ils trouvés?
10. En quoi n'as-tu plus confiance?

C. 1. Lequel de ces postes aimerais-tu?
2. Laquelle de ces voitures voudrait-il?
3. Laquelle de ces carrières choisiriez-vous?
4. Auxquels de ces étudiants est-ce que je préférerais téléphoner?
5. Lequel de ces conseils accepteriez-vous?
6. Desquels de ces messieurs parlaient-ils?
7. Lequel de ces cadeaux vous donnerait-elle?
8. De laquelle de ces facilitiés te servirais-tu?
9. Lequel de ces plats commanderait-il?
10. Auxquelles de ces œuvres vous intéresseriez-vous?

D. 1. ceux
2. celui
3. celle
4. ceux
5. celle
6. celui
7. celle/celle
8. celle/celle
9. celui
10. celui

E. 1. était partie
2. avions choisi
3. s'étaient servis
4. avais vu
5. avais suivi
6. m'étais souvenu(e)
7. avaient offert
8. aviez mis
9. était devenu
10. avaient écouté

F. 1. suis
2. suivez
3. suivons
4. Suis
5. suit
6. suivent
7. suivent
8. suis
9. suit
10. suivez

G. 1. Lequel des films aviez-vous déjà vu?
2. Vous devriez voir ceci! Suivez-moi!
3. Je ne sais pas si je devrais poursuivre ce poste-ci ou celui-là.
4. Elle avait suivi cinq cours l'année dernière. --Lequel était son préféré?
5. Le professeur m'a dit qu'elle s'était servie de mon idée. --De laquelle?
6. De quoi aviez-vous besoin pour aller à l'interview?
7. A qui pensez-vous?
8. Je vois plusieurs débouchés. --Auxquels vous intéressez-vous?
9. Nous ne croyons pas cela!
10. Ils aiment ma voiture mieux que celle de John.

I.

```
            E
            X
            C       S
      R E F U S E R        D I R E
      E     S   X          N
      M     E   C     S    V
      E         C  J U S T I F I E R
      R         S     L    T
      A C C E P T E R  E    E
      I         R     N    R
      E               C
    Ê T R E P O L I  E
                  G         B
                  N         O
                  O         I
              P R E N D R E
                  E         E
              M E R C I
```

II.

A.
1. serais allé(e)
2. aurait accepté
3. aurions pris
4. se seraient excusés
5. aurais remercié
6. auriez dit
7. se seraient amusés
8. aurais trouvé
9. auraient pu
10. serais revenu

B.
1. Si je l'avais trouvé odieux, j'aurais dit non.
2. Si la soirée dansante avait eu lieu ce soir, je n'aurais pas pu y aller.
3. S'il avait aimé la jeune fille, il l'aurait invitée à l'accompagner.
4. Si on avait servi de la bière, je n'en aurais pas bu.
5. Si le garçon l'avait invitée encore, elle aurait refusé.
6. Si nous avions voulu refuser, nous ne serions pas venus.
7. Si elles l'avaient trouvé sympa, elles l'auraient invité.
8. Si je l'avais détesté, je me serais excusé(e).

C. 1. Je me suis fait couper les cheveux.
   2. Elle fera préparer le repas.
   3. Nous ferions écrire l'invitation.
   4. Ils ont fait accepter la proposition.
   5. Vous faites faire vos valises.
   6. Tu as fait servir le punch.
   7. J'ai fait nettoyer ma chambre.
   8. Ils feront inviter leurs amis.
   9. Elle fera faire ses excuses.
  10. Vous ferez exprimer vos regrets.

D. 1. Ils le leur feront passer.
   2. Nous le leur avons fait faire.
   3. Tu la lui fais réparer.
   4. Je le leur avais fait
      apprendre.
   5. Vous les leur feriez chercher.
   6. Il la lui a fait accepter.
   7. Je les lui ferai offrir.
   8. Nous la leur avions fait
      nettoyer.

E. 1. En marchant, elle a vu un accident.
   2. Il parlait toujours en mangeant.
   3. Elle m'a beaucoup fâché en disant cela.
   4. En revenant du cinéma, il a rencontré un ancien ami.
   5. Vous vous êtes fait mal à la jambe en faisant du ski.
   6. Ils se sont rendu compte de leur erreur en écrivant la lettre.
   7. J'ai dû faire le plein en voyageant.
   8. Paul a marché sur son pied en dansant.
   9. On deviendra malade en fumant des cigarettes.
  10. Nous avons été très contents en ouvrant sa lettre.

F. 1. Buvez
   2. boivent
   3. bois
   4. boit
   5. buvons
   6. Bois
   7. boit
   8. boivent
   9. buvez
  10. buvons

G. 1. J'aurais fait laver ma voiture hier, mais il faisait mauvais.
   2. En rentrant du lycée, elle a perdu ses devoirs.
   3. Si j'avais su que vous aviez besoin de mon livre, je vous
      l'aurais envoyé.
   4. Il a fait apprendre un poème à ses étudiants.
   5. Nous aurions pris une boisson, mais nous n'avions pas soif.
   6. Ils auraient aimé aller à la soirée dansante.
   7. Je ne me moquerais pas de vous si je ne vous aimais pas.
   8. Seriez-vous restée si vous l'aviez voulu?
   9. Ils sont tombés amoureux en dansant.
  10. Je ferai vous téléphoner à Christophe quand il reviendra.

Chapitre Vingt-trois

I. 1. L'hôtesse (de l'air)
   2. éteindre/attacher/décoller/atterrir
   3. la douane/le douanier/fouille
   4. volent/prennent l'avion
   5. une carte d'embarquement

II.
A. 1. J'ai besoin des vôtres.
    2. A-t-il pris le sien?
    3. Le douanier a fouillé les siens.
    4. Nous montrons les nôtres.
    5. Elle a éteint la sienne.
    6. Vous avez attaché la vôtre.
    7. Ils attendaient le leur.
    8. Tu as mis les tiennes à la consigne.
    9. Elle ont rejoint les leurs.
   10. Il s'est intéressé aux miens.

B. 1. Les boissons ont été servies par l'hôtesse.
    2. Nos places seront choisies par nous.
    3. Mes bagages sont fouillés par le douanier.
    4. Il a été rejoint par ses amis.
    5. Leurs ceintures ont été attachées par leur mère.
    6. Le départ sera annoncé par une voix.
    7. Les repas ont déjà été préparés.
    8. L'avion est peint en bleu par eux.
    9. Les portes sont fermées par l'hôtesse.
   10. Les bagages ont été mis dans l'avion par les hommes.

C. 1. On a fouillé mes bagages.
    2. On annoncera l'arrivée.
    3. On occupe ma place.
    4. On nous rejoindra à l'aéroport.
    5. On prend leurs billets.
    6. On placera prudemment le bagage.
    7. Il faut qu'on attache les ceintures.
    8. On montrera la carte d'embarquement à l'hôtesse.
    9. On attend notre arrivée à New York.
   10. On réserve sa place.

D. 1. Voilà Jean dont le père est mon patron.
    2. As-tu le billet dont j'ai besoin?
    3. C'est l'atterrissage dont elle a peur.
    4. C'est notre pilote dont j'ai fait la connaissance.
    5. C'est l'heure du départ dont nous ne nous souvenons pas.
    6. C'est le Concorde dont j'ai entendu parler.
    7. C'est Jean dont vous avez pris la place.
    8. Voilà l'agent de voyages dont le fils est un de mes amis.
    9. C'est la date dont je ne me suis pas rendu compte.
   10. C'est ce monsieur-là dont tu a pris le magazine.

E. 1. Voilà l'aéroport où nous sommes arrivés.
    2. Connaissez-vous la ville où ils ont atterri?
    3. Voilà la porte où il faut attendre.
    4. C'est la salle où je t'ai attendu.
    5. C'est la place où elle a laissé son sac.
    6. Montrez-moi le café où vous l'avez aperçu.
    7. Voilà le kiosque où nous avons acheté les cartes.
    8. C'est le buffet où ils ont déjeuné.
    9. Où est l'agence de voyages où on fait les réservations?
   10. C'est cet avion-là où il est monté.

F. 1. ce qui   6. Ce qui
    2. ce dont   7. ce dont
    3. ce que   8. Ce dont
    4. ce qu'   9. ce qui
    5. ce que   10. ce que

G. 1. peignons   6. joins
    2. plains   7. craint
    3. se plaignent   8. Peint
    4. éteint   9. se plaignent
    5. rejoignez   10. Plaignez

H. 1. Le jour où je suis arrivé il faisait très froid, ce qui m'a
       surpris.
    2. Cette pièce a été peinte par mes étudiants. Est-ce que vos
       étudiants ont peint la vôtre?
    3. Le garçon dont on a volé la bicyclette est très triste. Je le
       plains.
    4. Nous venons de prendre nos billets. Ont-ils les leurs?
    5. Elle ne peut pas trouver la valise dont elle a besoin.
    6. Je crains qu'elle ait perdu ce qu'il faut avoir--son passeport.
    7. Ce que je n'aime pas, c'est le restaurant où nous avons mangé.
    8. Il était aimé de ses amis mais craint de ses étudiants.
    9. La bouteille avait été ouverte./On avait ouvert la bouteille.
   10. Savez-vous ce qui m'amuse? --Ce n'est pas ce qu'il dit mais
       comment il le dit.

SAMPLE TESTS

The following sample tests illustrate the variety of items that can be used in evaluating student mastery of grammar and acquired functional ability in the use of French.

With adequate classroom practice and drill and through periodic quizzing, the instructor can evaluate student mastery of paradigms and conjugations, i.e., the recall and accurate production of forms. Formal testing, on the other hand, need not call for exhaustive treatment of every form, structure, and exception. Instead, the test should call for the ready production of selected aspects of each grammar point in unexpected situations, thereby approximating real-language use. Such formal testing will then evaluate what students have learned and not memorized: material that is learned (internalized) can be used actively upon demand in unpredictable situations.

Evaluation of the speaking skill should be carried out in individual interview sessions with each students. Such sessions should last for no more than about ten minutes maximum.

Do not mix French and English in the same sentence. Such an item leads students to assume the one-to-one correlation of French and English vocabulary and structures.

The tests that follow should be used as guidelines and suggestions for the format of individual teacher-made tests. Remember: test what you have taught. Do not use formal testing for experimentation with new evaluative instruments that have not been practiced in class. For example, do not use translation of sentences from English to French if students have not practiced this skill, since translation is a special skill in itself.

Tests need not be based on a total score of 100, since each section should be weighted according to the emphasis given to each skill, and since answers to personalized and open-ended items are highly unpredictable and varied in length and complexity. In other words, do not let the total number of points on the test control the number of items and the length of the test. These sample tests can be completed satisfactorily in a 50-minute class meeting.

I. PARTIE ORALE

A. Do you hear le or la?

	LE	LA
1. Voilà le crayon.	___	___
2. C'est la femme.	___	___
3. Il n'a pas le livre.	___	___
4. Où est le musée?	___	___
5. Voici la banque.	___	___

B. Am I talking about one or more than one?

	ONE	MORE
1. Il a des disques.	___	___
2. J'aime les fruits.	___	___
3. As-tu un cahier?	___	___
4. Voilà des étudiants.	___	___
5. Il regarde l'homme.	___	___

C. Do you hear être or avoir?

	ETRE	AVOIR
1. Elle est jeune.	___	___
2. Ils ont du travail.	___	___
3. Tu es triste.	___	___
4. Ils sont au cinéma.	___	___
5. Nous sommes ici.	___	___

D. Do you hear a question or a statement?

	QUESTION	STATEMENT
1. Il est dans le parc.	___	___
2. Paul étudie-t-il la leçon?	___	___
3. As-tu de l'argent?	___	___
4. Ils n'ont pas de voiture.	___	___
5. Vous aimez le vin?	___	___

E. Complete the following sentences by filling in the blanks with the numbers you hear. Use arabic numerals.

1. Nous avons 5 classes.
2. Georges trouve 2 stylos.
3. Voilà 9 touristes américains.
4. J'ai 6 nouveaux disques.
5. Ils ouvrent 3 fenêtres.

F. Answer the following personal questions in complete French sentences.

1. Avez-vous un examen aujourd'hui?

   _____

2. Est-ce qu'il y a un restaurant à l'université?

   _____

3. Habitez-vous une résidence ici?

   _____

4. Avez-vous une voiture? Quelle est la couleur de la voiture?

   _____

II. PARTIE ECRITE

A. Fill in the blanks with the correct forms of the present indicative of the verbs indicated.

1. Quand je _____ à l'université, j'_____ des devoirs.
   ____(être)____   ____(avoir)____

2. Marie _____ la porte et _____ les étudiants qui
   ____(ouvrir)____   ____(regarder)____

   _____.
   __(jouer)__

3. _____-vous un crayon à l'étudiant?
   __(offrir)__

4. Paul et Hélène _____ en classe maintenant, mais ils
   ____(être)____

   _____ dans un instant.
   __(arriver)__

5. J'_____ que les garçons ne _____ pas anglais.
   __(oublier)__   ____(parler)____

B. Add the adjectives indicated to the following sentences and make all necessary changes.

1. (blanc, petit) Nous avons une voiture.

   _____

-143-

2. (nouveau) Qui est l'étudiant dans la classe?

_____

3. (vieux, français) Michel regarde des films.

_____

4. (beau, rouge) Ce sont des chaussures.

_____

5. (jeune, méchant) Je n'aime pas les enfants.

_____

C. Here are the answers to some questions. What questions were asked to get these answers?

1. _____?
   --Oui, nous cherchons le café.

2. _____?
   --Mais non, Christophe n'est pas laid!

3. _____?
   --Mais si, j'ai des devoirs!

4. _____?
   --Oui, il y a une piscine ici.

5. _____?
   --Non, la dame n'est pas chinoise.

D. Answer the following personal questions in complete French sentences.

1. Aimez-vous les plantes? Avez-vous des plantes dans la chambre?

_____

2. Habitez-vous ici dans la ville?

_____

3. Etes-vous américain(e)?

_____

4. Regardez-vous souvent la télévision?

_____

5. Avez-vous de vieux jeans?

   _____

E. Write five yes-no questions you would like to ask me.

   1. _____

   2. _____

   3. _____

   4. _____

   5. _____

I. PARTIE ORALE

A. Am I talking about all or only some?

	ALL	SOME
1. Je commande le vin.	___	___
2. Elle mange du pain.	___	___
3. Nous voulons les fruits.	___	___
4. Voudriez-vous de la salade?	___	___
5. Tu finis la viande.	___	___

B. Am I talking about one or several?

	ONE	SEVERAL
1. Regardez-vous le cheval?	___	___
2. Il va à l'hôpital.	___	___
3. Où sont les généraux?	___	___
4. Ils aiment les animaux.	___	___
5. As-tu leur journal?	___	___

C. Am I talking about un disque or une cassette--or can't you tell?

	DISQUE	CASSETTE	CAN'T TELL
1. Je le veux.	___	___	___
2. Nous l'écoutons.	___	___	___
3. Il la cherche.	___	___	___
4. Tu le demandes.	___	___	___
5. Vous l'aimez?	___	___	___

D. Am I talking about Paul or about Guy and Marie?

	PAUL	GUY ET MARIE
1. Il finit son travail.	___	___
2. Ils partent pour le cinéma.	___	___
3. Il dort en classe.	___	___
4. Il obéit au professeur.	___	___
5. Ils réussissent à l'examen.	___	___

E. Here is a chart of students studying various languages. Fill in the
chart with what you hear. Write arabic numerals.

	LANGUES		
	_____	_____	_____
garçons	____	____	____
jeunes filles	____	____	____
TOTAL	____	____	____

1. 14 étudiants étudient le latin:
   Il y a 9 jeunes filles et 5 garçons.

2. Il y a 19 étudiants en espagnol.
   Il y a 12 garçons et 7 jeunes filles.

3. Dans la classe de français, il y a 10 jeunes filles et 6 garçons.
   Le total est 16 étudiants.

(You may wish to read the sentences aloud a second time.)

II. PARTIE ECRITE

A. Fill in each blank with the correct preposition (+ definite article,
   if needed) to indicate <u>to</u>, <u>at</u>, <u>in</u>.

1. Philippe veut aller ___ Europe. Il va ___ France et ___ Pays-Bas.

2. Jacqueline voyage ___ Espagne et ___ Italie. Elle passe deux

   jours ___ Madrid.

3. Mes parents vont ___ Belgique. Puis ils vont ___ Luxembourg.

B. Rewrite the following sentences in the near future, saying that these
   things are going to be done tomorrow.

1. Nous allons en classe.

   _____

2. Je réponds à ta lettre.

   _____

3. Ils sont à Paris.

_____

4. Pars-tu demain?

_____

5. Vous rendez les livres à la bibliothèque.

_____

6. Anne offre de m'aider.

_____

C. Rewrite the following sentences, putting all nouns in the plural. Make all necessary changes.

1. Le fils offre un cadeau spécial à son neveu.

_____

2. Voilà un oiseau curieux!

_____

3. Voici un nouveau journal.

_____

D. Fill in the blanks with the appropriate possessive adjectives. Assume that the possessor is the subject of the sentence.

1. Les Dupont vont vendre ___ maison à ___ voisins.

2. Christophe perd ___ anorak et ___ chemise à l'ecole.

3. Nous préparons ___ devoirs pour ___ classe de mathématiques.

4. La jeune fille sert ___ dessert spécial à ___ ami Pierre.

5. J'offre ___ t-shirt à ___ sœur, parce qu'elle porte toujours ___ vêtements.

E. Compete the following sentences logically. Include the appropriate definite article or partitive article as needed.

1. Quand je vais dans un restaurant, je commande toujours ___, ___ et

___.

2. J'ai beaucoup ___ mais peu ___ .

3. Je ne mange pas ___ .

4. J'adore ___ et je déteste ___ .

F. Answer the following personal questions in complete sentences.

1. Aimez-vous regarder la télévision?

_____

2. Où voulez-vous voyager?

_____

3. Dormez-vous beaucoup?

_____

4. Aimez-vous votre camarade de chambre?

_____

5. Allez-vous travailler après l'école?

_____

I. PARTIE ORALE

A. Write the telephone numbers you hear.

1. Son numéro à Paris est <u>247-68-43</u>.

_____

2. A La Rochelle son numéro est <u>52-88-26</u>.

_____

3. Il habite Lyon et son numéro est <u>92-35-71</u>.

_____

4. Mon numéro à Bordeaux est <u>16-29-81</u>.

_____

B. Am I talking about <u>today</u> or <u>yesterday</u>?

	TODAY	YESTERDAY
1. Vous étudiez beaucoup.	___	___
2. Il a fini son dîner.	___	___
3. J'ai fait mon travail.	___	___
4. Nous avons pris sa voiture.	___	___
5. Ils vont au concert.	___	___

C. Am I talking about a <u>man</u> or a <u>woman</u>?

	MAN	WOMAN
1. Michelle est italienne.	___	___
2. René est gros.	___	___
3. Jeanne est française.	___	___
4. Daniel est indiscret.	___	___
5. Claude est heureuse.	___	___

D. Do you hear <u>faire</u> or <u>aller</u>?

	FAIRE	ALLER
1. Ils font du ski.	___	___
2. Je vais au concert.	___	___
3. Il fait de son mieux.	___	___
4. Tu vas en voyage.	___	___
5. Je fais des courses.	___	___

E. Do you hear a command or a statement?

	COMMAND	STATEMENT
1. Faites vos devoirs.	___	___
2. Vous parlez bien.	___	___
3. Sois sérieux!	___	___
4. Répondons au téléphone.	___	___
5. Philippe, obéis-moi!	___	___

II. PARTIE ECRITE

A. Write out the following times in both conventional and 24-hour time:

1. 1:45 AM _____

2. 12:30 PM _____

3. 4:03 PM _____

4. 11:59 AM _____

5. 6:15 PM _____

B. Rewrite the following commands in the negative:

1. Donnez-le-moi. _____

2. Demandez-les-lui. _____

3. Montrez-la nous. _____

4. Prenez-les leur. _____

C. Answer the following personal questions, using indirect object pronouns:

1. Ecrivez-vous souvent à vos parents?

_____

2. Est-ce que vos parents vous téléphonent?

_____

3. Parlez-vous aux autres étudiants en classe?

_____

4. Prêtez-vous vos notes à votre camarade de chambre?

_____

5. Aimez-vous rendre visite à vos amis?

_____

D. Rewrite the following sentences, putting all verbs in the passé composé.

1. Ma mère fait des courses aujourd'hui.

_____

2. L'homme trouve une jolie fleur et il la donne à sa femme.

_____

3. Aprés le voyage, nous prenons du café et nous dormons douze heures.

_____

4. Comprends-tu la léçon que tu étudies?

_____

5. Les étudiants rendent leurs devoirs au professeur, mais il ne les corrige pas.

_____

6. J'offre un cadeau à mon ami, mais il ne l'accepte pas.

_____

E. Answer the following personal questions.

1. Venez-vous de déjeuner?

_____

2. Quel temps fait-il aujourd'hui?

_____

3. A quelle heure commence cette classe?

_____

4. Aimez-vous étudier le français? Pourquoi?

_____

5. Avez-vous assisté à un concert de musique rock?

   _____

6. Quand téléphonez-vous à vos parents?

   _____

F. Write five sentences saying what you did yesterday.

   1. _____

   2. _____

   3. _____

   4. _____

   5. _____

I. PARTIE ORALE

A. Do you hear <u>être</u> or <u>avoir</u> as auxiliary verbs?

	ETRE	AVOIR
1. Ils sont allés en Franc.	___	___
2. Elle a appris le français.	___	___
3. Tu as sorti de l'argent.	___	___
4. Nous sommes arrivés en classe.	___	___
5. Etes-vous entré dans le métro?	___	___

B. Do you hear the <u>passé composé</u> or the <u>imperfect</u>?

	PASSE COMPOSE	IMPERFECT
1. J'étudiais beaucoup en high school	___	___
2. Tu as été malade.	___	___
3. Il a dit oui.	___	___
4. Nous savions nager.	___	___
5. Ils allaient à la plage.	___	___

C. Are the verbs you hear reflexive or not reflexive?

	REFLEXIVE	NOT REFLEXIVE
1. Je me lave les cheveux.	___	___
2. Ils disent bonjour.	___	___
3. Réveillez-vous!	___	___
4. Jean et Françoise se parlent.	___	___
5. Tu t'arrêtes de travailler.	___	___

D. Do you hear <u>dire</u>, <u>lire</u>, or <u>écrire</u>?

	DIRE	LIRE	ECRIRE
1. Il lit un journal.	___	___	___
2. Nous disons nos noms.	___	___	___
3. Tu écris une lettre.	___	___	___
4. Ils lisent la phrase.	___	___	___
5. J'écris un télégramme.	___	___	___

II. PARTIE ECRITE

A. Rewrite the underlined verbs in the <u>passé composé</u> or the imperfect in the numbered blanks following the text.

Un étudiant américain <u>vient</u> (1) d'arriver en France. Il ne <u>parle</u> (2) pas bien le français. Puisqu'il <u>a</u> (3) faim, il <u>entre</u> (4) dans un petit restaurant. Il n'y <u>a</u> (5) pas de table libre, et il <u>prend</u> (6) une place à une table avec un Français qui ne <u>parle</u> (7) pas du tout

l'anglais. Le Français lui _dit_ (8) <<bon appétit!>> L'étudiant
répond (9): <<John Smith.>> Après le repas, le Français _part_ (10).

Le lendemain l'étudiant _se trouve_ (11) de nouveau au même restaurant-
-et voilà le même Français qui _prend_ (12) son déjeuner. L'étudiant
se met (13) à la même table. Le Français lui _dit_ (14) encore <<Bon
appétit!>>. Et l'étudiant, qui _ne comprend pas_ (15) ce que le
monsieur _dit_ (16), _répond_ (17): <<John Smith.>>

Le soir, l'étudiant _raconte_ (18) l'histoire à un ami qui _est_ (19)
trés amusé. L'ami lui _explique_ (20) que le Français _veut_ (21) être
poli.

L'étudiant _va_ (22) encore au même restaurant. Il _cherche_ (23) le
Français. Le voilà! Il _marche_ (24) vers la table. Quand il _arrive_
(25) à la table, il _a_ (26) beaucoup de confiance quand il _dit_ (27)
<<Bon appétit!>> au Français. Le monsieur _se lève_ (28), et confiant
lui aussi, _serre_ (29) la main à l'étudiant et _prononce_ (30) <<John
Smith!>>

1. _____   16. _____
2. _____   17. _____
3. _____   18. _____
4. _____   19. _____
5. _____   20. _____
6. _____   21. _____
7. _____   22. _____
8. _____   23. _____
9. _____   24. _____
10. _____   25. _____
11. _____   26. _____
12. _____   27. _____
13. _____   28. _____
14. _____   29. _____
15. _____   30. _____

B. Translate the following sentences into French:

1. How long have you been here? --I've been here two weeks.

_____

2. Paul had just got home when the phone rang.

_____

3. Michel and I are going to the movies with our friends. Do you
   want to go with us?

_____

_____

C. Answer the following questions:

1. Depuis combien de temps étudiez-vous le français?

_____

2. Quel âge avez-vous?

_____

3. A quelle heure vous réveillez-vous d'habitude?

_____

4. Avez-vous peur de votre professeur de français?

_____

5. Voulez-vous vous marier? Pourquoi (pas)?

_____

D. Complete each sentence with an adjective + noun to complete the definition:

1. Une femme qui n'a pas d'argent est _____.

2. La semaine qui précède cette semaine est _____.

3. Un de mes professeurs de high school est _____.

4. Le travail que j'ai fait moi-même est _____.

E. Give the adverbs related to the following adjectives:

1. bon _____

2. constant _____

3. franc _____

4. vrai _____

5. malheureux _____

F. Complete the following partial translations, using the correct emphatic pronouns:

1. Did Jacques and you prepare the meal? No, it was she.

   Est-ce que Jacques et _____, vous avez préparé le repas?

   --Non, c'était _____.

2. Who broke the window?   --He did!

   Qui a cassé la fenêtre? _____!

3. That book is hers, not mine.

   Ce livre est à _____, pas à _____.

4. <u>You</u> don't know, do you?

   _____, tu ne sais pas, hein?

I. PARTIE ORALE

A. Do you hear the <u>future</u> tense or the <u>present</u>?

	FUTURE	PRESENT
1. Il fera ses devoirs.	___	___
2. Nous finirons notre travail.	___	___
3. Je vais au théâtre ce soir.	___	___
4. Vous vendrez votre voiture.	___	___
5. Ils sont en retard.	___	___

B. Do you hear <u>pouvoir</u> or <u>vouloir</u>?

	POUVOIR	VOULOIR
1. Il peut partir.	___	___
2. Je ne peux pas rester.	___	___
3. Nous voulons réussir.	___	___
4. Elles ne peuvent pas entendre.	___	___
5. Veux-tu m'accompagner?	___	___

C. Am I asking a question about a <u>person</u> or a <u>thing</u>?

	PERSON	THING
1. Que voulez-vous?	___	___
2. Qui vient ce soir?	___	___
3. Qu'est-ce qui se passe?	___	___
4. Qui est-ce que tu connais ici?	___	___
5. Qu'est-ce qu'il cherche?	___	___

D. Am I talking about <u>one</u> or <u>more than one</u>?

	ONE	MORE THAN ONE
1. J'adore ces pulls.	___	___
2. Prenez-vous ce train?	___	___
3. Que dit cette femme?	___	___
4. Nous n'aimons pas ces desserts.	___	___
5. Veux-tu ce journal?	___	___

II. PARTIE ECRITE

A. Combine the following sentences by rewriting them with the appropriate relative pronouns.

1. J'ai vu un nouveau film. Je l'ai beaucoup aimé.

_____

2. Elle a rencontré un vieil ami. Il l'a saluée.

_____

3. Il achète une chemise. Elle lui va bien.

_____

4. As-tu trouvé tes clés? Tu les as perdues hier.

_____

5. Jacques a aimé le cadeau. Nous le lui avons envoyé.

_____

B. Here is a conversation in which all the questions are missing. Create appropriate questions to complete the conversation.

Paul.   Salut, Guy. _____?

Guy.   Je pense aller à la plage. _____?

Paul.   Je voudrais bien t'accompagner, mais je ne peux pas.

Guy.   _____?

Paul.   Il me faut préparer un examen. _____?

Guy.   Henri et Luc viennent avec moi.

Paul.   _____?

Guy.   Nous allons y rester toute la journée.

Paul.   _____?

Guy.   Nous prenons la voiture de Luc.

Paul.   _____?

Guy.   Nous rentrons probablement vers 8h du soir.

Paul.   Ah, oui? Alors, j'y vais. _____?

Guy.   Tu peux apporter des sandwiches et une bouteille de vin, d'accord?

C. Fill in the blanks with the correct form of the present indicative of the infinitives given.

1. Comment _____? Je _____ Jean Penaud.
     (s'appeler)   (s'appeler)

-159-

2. Elle _____ prendre le train quand nous _____ en Europe.
   (préférer)   (voyager)

3. Si vous _____ votre chambre, votre mère vous _____.
           (nettoyer)   (payer)
   cinq dollars?

4. Paul _____ une carte postale qu'il _____ à ses parents.
        (acheter)   (envoyer)

D. Fill in the blanks with the present indicative of <u>savoir</u> or <u>connaître</u> as determined by the context.

1. _____-vous l'adresse de Jean-Luc? --Jean-Luc? Je ne

   le _____ pas!

2. Je ne _____ pas que faire aujourd'hui.

3. Nous _____ qu'elle est partie avec quelqu'un mais nous

   ne _____ pas où elle va.

4. _____-il bien Paris?

E. Answer the following questions, using <u>y</u> or <u>en</u>.

1. Combien de frères avez-vous?

   _____

2. Etes-vous jamais allé(e) à la plage?

   _____

3. Répondez-vous toujours au téléphone quand il sonne?

   _____

4. Venez-vous de cet état?

   _____

5. Avez-vous réussi au dernier examen de français?

   _____

F. Complete the following sentences:

1. Je serai heureux/heureuse quand _____

2. Mon père est un homme que _____.

3. Si j'ai le temps ce weekend, je (j') _____.

4. Je suis content(e) parce que je peux _____.

5. Ce soir je me coucherai aussitôt que _____.

Chapitres 16-18

I. PARTIE ORALE

A. Do you hear the _future_ or the _conditional_?

	FUTURE	CONDITIONAL
1. Nous irions avec toi.	___	___
2. Tu voudras en prendre.	___	___
3. Ils vous aiderait.	___	___
4. Vous en serez content.	___	___
5. Marie viendrait te voir.	___	___

B. Do you hear _mieux_ or _meilleur_?

	MIEUX	MEILLEUR
1. Il chante mieux que moi.	___	___
2. Ce programme est le meilleur.	___	___
3. Qui conduit mieux?	___	___
4. C'est le meilleur travail.	___	___
5. Ces fleurs sentent meilleurs.	___	___

C. Write the fractions you hear, using arabic numerals.

1. 3/4 _____

2. 9/11 _____

3. 1/2 _____

4. 2/3 _____

5. 4/7 _____

D. Are these sentences _affirmative_ or _negative_?

	AFFIRMATIVE	NEGATIVE
1. Etes-vous jamais allée en France?	___	___
2. Connaissez-vous cette personne?	___	___
3. Elle n'a plus d'examens.	___	___
4. Nous ne voyons rien.	___	___
5. Il ne veut pas me parler.	___	___

E. Do you hear the _comparative_ or the _superlative_?

	COMPARATIVE	SUPERLATIVE
1. Paul est le plus riche.	___	___
2. Elle est moins intelligente.	___	___
3. Je suis le plus diligent.	___	___
4. Ce disque est plus cher.	___	___
5. Son livre est mieux écrit.	___	___

II. PARTIE ECRITE

A. Combine the two sentences, using the subjunctive or an infinitive construction as required.

1. Elle m'écrit. J'en suis heureux.

_____

2. Tu partiras demain. Le faut-il?

_____

3. Nous y allons avec le groupe. Nous le voulons.

_____

4. Elles ne peuvent pas venir. Elles en sont tristes.

_____

5. Je fais tout mon travail. Le professeur le doute.

_____

B. Rewrite the following sentences in the negative, making them say exactly the opposite. Make all necessary changes.

1. Ils arrivent toujours en retard.

_____

2. Les touristes prennent encore des photos.

_____

3. Quelqu'un t'a téléphoné.

_____

4. J'ai acheté quelque chose de trés cher.

_____

5. Elle a beaucoup de travail à faire.

_____

C. Complete the following sentences:

1. Mes parents veulent que je _____.

2. Je doute que mon/ma camarade de chambre _____ .

3. Après la classe, il faut que je _____ .

4. Ma mère est très heureuse que je _____ .

5. Pour réussir dans ce cours, il est indispensable _____ .

D. Complete the following sentences:

1. Si on me donnait une nouvelle voiture, _____ .

2. _____ si j'étudiais en France.

3. Si j'avais l'occasion, _____ .

E. Write a sentence about each subject using the positive, comparative, and superlative degrees of the adjectives or adverbs given.

1. moi, mon père, ma mère (grand)

_____

2. un homme, une femme, un(e) adolescent(e) (conduire bien)

_____

3. l'anglais, le français, le chinois (être difficile)

_____

F. Answer the following questions in French:

1. A quel étage se trouve la salle de classe?

_____

2. Connaissez-vous quelqu'un de célèbre?

_____

3. Que feriez-vous si vous obteniez un A à cet examen?

_____

4. Que voulez-vous que le professeur fasse?

_____

5. L'admettez-vous quand vous avez tort?

_____

Chapitres 19-21

I. PARTIE ORALE

A. Am I talking about a person or a thing?

	PERSON	THING
1. A qui parlez-vous?	___	___
2. De quoi a-t-il besoin?	___	___
3. Pour qui votes-tu?	___	___
4. Sur quoi comptez-vous?	___	___
5. A qui pensent-ils?	___	___

B. Am I talking about Monique or Robert?

	MONIQUE	ROBERT
1. C'est une étudiante.	___	___
2. Il est Américain.	___	___
3. Elle est à l'université.	___	___
4. C'est mon cousin.	___	___
5. Il est gentil.	___	___

C. Am I talking about one or more than one?

	ONE	MORE THAN ONE
1. Lesquels voudriez-vous?	___	___
2. A laquelle penses-tu?	___	___
3. Lequel ce ces livres a-t-il écrit?	___	___
4. Desquels ont-ils besoin?	___	___
5. Derrière laquelle marche-t-il?	___	___

D. Do you hear the pluperfect or the passé composé?

	PLUPERFECT	P.C.
1. Il m'avait vu au cinéma.	___	___
2. Vous avez parlé au vendeur.	___	___
3. Elle était sortie sans lui.	___	___
4. Es-tu descendu du train?	___	___
5. Nous n'avions pas compris la question.	___	___

E. Were these people supposed to do what is mentioned or should they do it?

	SUPPOSED TO	SHOULD
1. Nous devions choisir un job.	___	___
2. Il devrait se lever.	___	___
3. Je devais passer un examen.	___	___
4. Vous deviez m'attendre.	___	___
5. Tu devrais rendre visite à ton frère.	___	___

II. PARTIE ECRITE

A. Fill in the blanks with the appropriate forms of the demonstrative pronouns.

1. J'aime bien cet appartement-ci, mais je déteste _____.

2. Connais-tu Maria et Franz? _____ est allemand, _____ est suédoise.

3. Les hommes qui réuississent sont _____ qui travaillent le plus.

B. Combine the pairs of sentences, using the suggested conjunction or preposition as needed.

1. Il est rentré tard. Sa mère ne le savait pas. (sans, sans que)

_____

2. Je le répéterai. Vous l'entendrez. (pour, pour que)

_____

3. Vous devriez préparer l'examen. Vous recevrez une mauvaise note. (de peur de, de peur que)

_____

C. Complete the following sentences with the past subjunctive of the infinitives given.

1. C'est dommage qu'elle _____ aller avec toi.
   (ne pas pouvoir)

2. Nous avions peur que vous _____.
   (partir)

3. Paul était arrivé chez Jacqueline avant qu'elle _____.
   (se lever)

D. Answer the following questions in French.

1. Combien de cours suivez-vous?

_____

2. Quel cours préférez-vous?

_____

3. A quoi vous intéressez-vous?

_____

4. Aviez-vous étudié le français avant de venir à l'université?

_____

E. Translate the following sentences:

1. I must have lost my notebook. --Which one? --The one you gave me yesterday.

_____

2. The pen you're writing with is mine.

_____

3. Do you know anyone who knows how to speak Russian?

_____

4. Which (one) of these roads is the best?

_____

5. You ought to pay attention! It's a shame you didn't understand that.

_____

F. Combine the pairs of sentences, using the appropriate relative pronouns.

1. C'est un candidat. Je ne voterais jamais pour lui.

_____

2. Voilà un débouché. Il y pense depuis des années.

_____

3. Qui est la dame? Vous vous trouviez à côté d'elle.

_____

4. As-tu trouvé les cartes? Tu en avais besoin.

_____

I. PARTIE ORALE

A. Are the sentences you hear <u>active</u> or <u>passive</u>?

	ACTIVE	PASSIVE
1. Il a été bien reçu.	—	—
2. Je suis sorti à midi.	—	—
3. L'avion est vide.	—	—
4. Le dîner est servi.	—	—
5. Ses bagages ont été fouillés.	—	—

B. Am I talking about <u>one</u> or <u>more than one</u>?

	ONE	MORE THAN ONE
1. As-tu les tiens?	—	—
2. Ils m'ont montré la leur.	—	—
3. Où est la sienne?	—	—
4. Je ne peux pas trouver les miens.	—	—
5. Nous aurions vendu le nôtre.	—	—

C. Did these people <u>do</u> these things or <u>have them done</u>?

	DO	HAVE DONE
1. Je me fais couper les cheveux.	—	
2. Il a lavé sa voiture.	—	—
3. Nous avons fait envoyer un télégramme.		
4. Faites venir le médecin.	—	—
5. Ils ont fait tous leurs devoirs.	—	—

D. Circle the present participle.

1. voyageons   voyageant   voyageons

2. sachant   sachons   sachons

3. allons   allant   allons

4. finissons   finissons   finissant

5. ayant   ayons   ayons

II. PARTIE ECRITE

A. Complete the following sentences with the correct tense of the infinitives given.

1. Paul _____ s'il avait été invité.
     (rester)

2. Si je n'avais pas su la réponse, je _____ la main.
                                              (ne pas lever)

3. Jacques _____ en vacances s'il n'avait pas eu de travail.
            (aller)

B. Rewrite the following sentences in the passive voice. If there is no passive equivalent, write "No passive."

1. Le père de Robert lui a téléphoné.

   _____

2. Ses étudiants l'aiment beaucoup.

   _____

3. Le douanier a fouillé mes bagages.

   _____

4. Le conseiller lui a suggéré un job.

   _____

C. Combine each pair of sentences with the appropriate relative pronoun.

1. Je n'ai jamais vu la pièce. Vous en parlez.

   _____

2. Il voudrait voir l'appartement. Ils y passent leurs vacances.

   _____

3. Nous avons fait la connaissance du garçon. Son père est journaliste.

   _____

4. Qui est le professeur? Tu as peur de lui.

   _____

D. Translate the following sentences:

1. I don't understand what you're saying.

   _____

2. French is spoken in Louisiana.

   _____

3. While taking a walk, he saw an accident.

   _____

4. He had the travel agent prepare a trip for him.

   _____

5. I would have been surprised if you had said that.

   _____

E. Answer the following questions in complete sentences:

1. Que buvez-vous d'habitude au dîner?

   _____

2. Qui avez-vous rencontré en venant en classe?

   _____

3. Qui craignez-vous?

   _____

4. Que craignez-vous?

   _____

F. Fill in the blanks with ce qui, ce que, ce dont:

1. Voici _____ est important: c'est d'étudier.

2. Dis-moi _____ tu as peur.

3. _____ vous dites et _____ vous faites sont
   tout à fait différents.